LEARNING TO WALK AGAIN

Rethinking Just About Everything I Know

Jeffrey Cook

D1512171

To Inge

Love of my life

"Sometimes I have felt like a man climbing in the darkness a winding staircase in the steeple of an ancient cathedral. In the blackness I reached out to steady myself and my hand laid hold of a rope. I was startled to hear the clanging of a bell."
Karl Barth

Table of Contents

Preface..9

Introduction..12

I. NEIGHBORS 15

But You Can't Raise a Family There!.............................. 16

One Mile Radius... 17

Transitions... 18

Living on the Edge 21

Friends and Neighbors 22

What Took You So Long? 23

Who I Want to Be at 86... 24

You Buy for Me, Yes? 25

Why I Don't Cut My Neighbor's Lawn 26

Judge Tyrone 28

Praying in the Front Yard.. 29

McDonald's at 7:00 a.m. 30

At the Goodwill.. 31

Loved and Wanted 32

Alone 34

II. FAMILY..37

Sunday Evenings 38

Overcoming Fear.. 39

A Healing Community 41

Grieving in Community 42

The Swing of the Pendulum 45

Promptings 47

A Theology of Hanging Out... 48

Cleaning Up a Mess 49

Speaking Life 50

The Sovereignty of God 51

God's Protection.. 53

Learning Curve... 54

III. LOVED AND WANTED 57

William on Colfax... 58

Welcome Home... 60

Thanks for Talking to Us 61

Community... 63

We're All Broken 64

First You Have to See 64

No Drive-By Ministry 65

Please Don't Give Me a Christian Cellmate 67

Nowhere to Go 68

Impossible 69

I'll Find My Way... 70

Full Circle.. 73

What Are Your Addictions?... 75

On Reaching Muslims... 76

IV. NEW LENSES..79

Can You Help Me?.. 80

Helping Without Insulting... 81

Who Exactly Are the Poor?... 82

Context 83

Doing Church Right 84

Poverty of Trusting People.. 86

Thundering Herd 86

Thundering Herd II.. 88

Slow Growth 90

Worth It 92

You Can't Rush Understanding 93

Winter.. 95

Living with No Answers 96

Pulling Back the Curtain 97

Pain in the Offering 98

Waiting 100

V. BEAUTY AND BROKENNESS.......................................103

You Gotta Know This Place to Fix It................................ 104

What Do You See?.. 104

On Fixing People... 105

Why We Stayed 106

Investing 108

Bonsai Ministry 109

Power and Injustice 110

You Can't Un-see... 111

Help and Hope After Prison 112

Invisible Injustice 114

When Sin Is More Than Personal 115

Polaroid Ministry.. 117

VI. DEEP ROOTS 119

Expectations 120

Slow Down.. 120

Who Is Fixing Whom? 121

The Price of Ministry 123

Doubt.. 124

No Smell of Smoke 126

Saying Goodbye 128

Ministry Is Hard 129

Dark Night of the Soul 130

Team Player 133

Leaving Church 134

Throwing Good Money After Bad 135

All I've Got 136

Traveling the Back Roads 136

Sometimes He Delivers 139

Show Us Something New? 140

Paying Attention 141

Twenty One Principles for Living 142

Afterword 145

Acknowledgements 147

Preface

I quit high school and joined the Army in 1971, one week past my seventeenth birthday. It probably was not the smartest decision of my life. Anxious to be on my own, adrift and chafing at the authority of my parents as a teenager, I must have thought in the military I wouldn't have to submit to anyone. I was a bit confused.

I thought of myself as a tough guy and was more than ready to leave my immature high school environment far behind, but when I tried to enlist for Viet Nam I discovered you had to be eighteen to volunteer for combat. When I asked where the next farthest place away from home was, the recruiter said he could send me to Germany, so I signed up. He never asked why.

I was primed for a big challenge and so volunteered for Airborne school in Georgia. No more high school for me. I became a U.S. Army paratrooper, and those silver jump wings on my chest only fueled the pride and arrogance in my heart.

Unfortunately, when I bolted from home I took myself with me. It took me two years to come to the end of myself as a hard drinking, dope-smoking, tough-guy paratrooper on his own in the middle of Europe. I fell in love with a young German girl named Inge, and we married when I was 19 and she just 17.

That is a statement, not a recommendation. (We're still married, 42 years later!).

A year into our marriage we both came to faith in Jesus, and God turned our lives around so drastically that after seven years in the

Army, I got out and invested the next several years in training for the ministry in a conservative, evangelical Bible college and seminary.

Following graduation we wrestled with what the next career step was for us, and we concluded that the only thing we knew was Europe and the military. We returned as church-planting missionaries to the military, and spent the next ten years planting and pastoring two American military churches in Germany. I never expected to do anything else.

Because of some success in church planting, however, I was invited to return to the U.S. and teach at an inner-city Bible college with a very non-traditional student body. Almost all were older African-American pastors with families who were already shepherding churches. It was then I discovered, surprisingly, that I had been very well prepared academically and theologically for ministry, but only as long as the context was suburban, middle-class, white America. I was woefully unprepared outside of that. Almost nothing I had learned in college or seminary had prepared me socially or culturally for this new environment, and that was the beginning of a scramble to learn a holistic, culturally informed philosophy of ministry that was adequate for the city and poverty. The learning curve was frightfully steep.

Deeply disappointing was the realization that all of my training had been solely within the theological and philosophical framework of white, middle-class North American and European theologians. Furthermore, my philosophy of ministry was shaped by a church-centered, dominant-culture methodology that de-emphasized social context and structures and focused almost exclusively on the spiritual. Although it had been previously invisible to me, I came to see that I had absorbed a single model of ministry in my formal training that was woefully inadequate for the multi-ethnic context of poverty where I now found myself.

I had to begin to learn to walk all over again and re-think almost everything I had learned while preparing for ministry. If I was going to be effective now, I would have to develop a philosophy of ministry that was both culturally and theologically informed for the poor, urban, multi-ethnic context.

I will be forever grateful for the friendship and support of so many fellow African-American pastors and friends who walked along side of me, taught me, often corrected me, and encouraged me for fifteen years as I served alongside of them. Those were profoundly formative years, and my life and ministry have been infinitely richer because of their investment in my life.

Three years ago Inge and I moved to Denver, Colorado, to serve with Providence Bible Church and CrossPurpose Center for Urban Leadership. It is a multi-ethnic, holistic ministry deeply committed to eliminating relational, spiritual and economic poverty in the neighborhoods where we serve. It is a gift of God at this stage of life, and the capstone of a life of ministry to be able to pour our lives out alongside these brothers and sisters. God has been good to me.

The following snapshots reflect broadly the outworking of the holistic model I have learned in the multi-ethnic trenches of urban ministry.

Jeff Cook

Denver, 2016

Introduction

"If our theology doesn't shift and change over our lifetimes, then I have to wonder if we're paying attention. The Spirit is often breathing in the very changes or shifts that used to terrify us."
Sarah Bessey

My friend remarked recently that he was a much better husband before he was married.

I knew what he meant. It mirrors my journey in the ministry as well. I was a much better pastor and theologian back when I was young and knew everything, back before I was ordained and had actually shepherded some of God's flock. Dr. Chuck Swindoll understood that when he said it took him four years to get through seminary and ten years to get over it.

It's not that I don't have theological convictions now at this age. I do. I am more convinced now than ever of some truth, much of which has been gained in life and ministry with Jesus and people in the trenches. On the other hand, there are many theological hills I am not willing to die on now that I have been around the block a few times. I no longer feel compelled to hang my four earned theological degrees prominently on my office wall to prove that I am smart and credentialed in the right theological camp. I no longer feel the need to "defend the faith", I now am much more inclined to continually deepen and broaden my understanding of it.

The more we learn, the more we realize how little we know. The last four decades in ministry have tempered the unshakeable confidence I had earlier in my formal training. Oh, I still value the training I received; I just realize now it was the starting point of my education and not the conclusion. It is no longer the ultimate and unchangeable grid through which I evaluate everything else. God I trust implicitly, theological systems maybe not so much.

My years in ministry have served to expand and deepen my understanding, and to embrace a God and his agenda that is much broader than I could have ever imagined previously in my Americanized, denominational, fundamentalist, provincial view of the Kingdom. The journey has been both enlightening and profoundly humbling.

At the core of my being is a bedrock conviction that Jesus is God and we all need reconciliation and restoration to him by grace alone through faith alone in his death and resurrection.

Beyond that, I have come to rethink and embrace a much broader philosophy of ministry; a balanced, integrated holistic view of spiritual and social ministry. Like two wings on an airplane, both are necessary. It is meaningless, in my opinion, to insist that one is more important than the other, in the same way it is nonsense to insist that one wing on an airplane is more important than the other. Human beings are created spiritually and physically integrated "wholes" who exist in community. Many of the following reflections highlight the value and necessity of ministering to people from that vantage point.

Furthermore, as you peruse these reflections you will see that I have tried to highlight not only the profound value of all people regardless of their socio-economic strata, culture, nationality, theological stance or ethnicity, but also the astonishing breadth, width and depth of the family of God as well. The frontiers of my thinking have been pushed out significantly compared to my earlier years and background.

I am even more deeply committed at this stage of life to the high value of racial diversity and the pursuit of justice. I agree with those who would say that Satan gets more mileage out of the exploitation of race in the Church and in America than any other issue. The pressing need for us as the American church is to figure it out, in the same way that the early church had to figure out and work through their Jew-Gentile issues. Neither Jesus nor Paul ever settled for a "separate but equal" church, and we must also refuse to settle for an uneasy tolerance or cease-fire simply because it is a knotty issue. The Body is enriched by healthy diversity, and it is a powerful reflection on the nature of God to a watching society. On the other hand, the Body is also robbed of power and its testimony when it gets its cues more from a polarized, racist society than from Scripture. I long to see us do better.

Finally, the clear calling of the Church to embrace the poor is also foundational in my growing understanding of our mission as followers of Jesus. God's heart for the poor seems to leak out of nearly every chapter of the Bible, and yet it has only been in recent years that I have begun to see beyond the narrow parameters of a certain stance that viewed the poor more from a political platform than Scripture. We must embrace and engage the poor much as the fire department does houses on fire. They are wholly committed to everyone in the neighborhood, but they are most concerned about those with the greatest needs. That compassionate view, I trust, flows out of the following reflections as well.

I have loosely grouped these social media writings from the last several years around certain core values I have come to embrace at this stage of my life and ministry. *Neighbors* reflects our deep commitment and the rich relationships we share with our geographical neighbors. *Family* show what the relationships within our spiritual family look like as we live them out in community. *Loved and Wanted* centers around stories of interaction and bridge-building with those in our larger community that we so value and love in the flow of urban life. In *New Lenses* I have tried to communicate some of the broader issues surrounding cultural competency that are so necessary to minister effectively in the city. *Beauty and Brokenness* captures snapshots of the social realities of the urban community that makes it both so painful and yet so attractive to invest one's life and family here. Finally, in *Deep Roots* I have tried to articulate some of the practical theology that informs an authentic life of service poured out to God. They are not all exclusively focused on urban life, many reflect simply attempts at living and growing purposefully in Christ.

I continue to listen for the voice of God in the flow of life and ministry and then write what I am learning. My prayer is that some of this will resonate with you.

I. NEIGHBORS

But You Can't Raise a Family There!

Confronting the Idols of Safety and Security

I have taught urban ministry and world missions for over twenty years at the university level, and I have seen a particular scenario play out so regularly it is a recognizable pattern. The Spirit of God will move in particular students over the course of a semester as we study God's heart for the poor and marginalized, and a deep concern will begin to grow in them. At some point they will have a long, heart-felt conversation with family or others who love them about their growing desire to invest their lives among the poor and disenfranchised, but the sudden resistance is shocking to them.

They eventually trek to my office at some point, deeply confused.

"I have been raised in a Christian home," they will say, "and have been taught to love God, commit my life to him and live in obedience to him. Yet now as I tell them what I believe God is doing in my heart and my desire to follow his leading, they push back and strongly try to discourage me from doing it. Suddenly their confidence in God leading me evaporates when it is different than what they envisioned."

Releasing a loved one to the leading of the Spirit can be terrifying, particularly if it means the danger or the unknown. Fear shakes many a person's theology and trust in God.

How astonishing that Jesus chose to leave his upscale, posh, gated community of heaven and physically move into our run-down, violent neighborhood called Earth, so full of desperate problems and broken people.

Did well-meaning angels give him advice "for his own good" before he moved to earth? Did they sit him down, lean in closer and talk in serious, measured tones about how dangerous it was, how violent, how dirty, how corrupt?

"You can't raise a family there you know," they might have warned solemnly. "Listen to reason, Jesus. We want what's best for you. It's not wise. A person could get killed there."

Apparently Jesus believed that Truth is not just a sterile, neat package of theological content to be drop-shipped. If his actions mean anything, he was convinced that Truth needed to be poured out through long term, life-on-life relationships, even in the midst of difficulty and messiness. Rather than modeling drive-by ministry, Jesus showed us what it looks like to invest in people by leading an incarnational, downwardly mobile lifestyle.

How many of us, if we had been among his heavenly contemporaries, would have counseled Jesus against the incarnation?

Those of us who have chosen to follow the call of God to invest their lives in difficult and poor communities have heard this well-meaning warning many times, often from those closest to us. We understand the spirit of it. We know it flows from a heart of love and concern, but it also flows from a heart of paralyzing fear. If we are not careful, we easily lose our theology at the prospect of downward mobility or risk-taking.

Courage! You are immortal until your work on earth is done.
George Whitefield

One Mile Radius

"Good neighbors always spy on you to make sure you are doing well."
Pawan Mishra

Ninety-eight percent of our lives now takes place within a one mile radius here in Denver. We love it. It hasn't always been this way. There have been times we lived places where we spent half of our lives in our car. This has caused us to rethink how we live our lives. Here's what I mean:

Jesus "became flesh and dwelt among them." He left his neighborhood, moved into our broken, dangerous, violent neighborhood called Earth and lived life together with people. That model of incarnational and purposeful living in community is refreshing as well as revolutionary to us.

Most often it seems that those who fear the city are those who don't live here. When you plant yourself here, you find that close proximity to neighbors provides natural connections. We share meals. We help each other move heavy furniture, we do yard work together. Sometimes we barbecue, and other times we cut each other's grass. At Christmas-time we serenade each other with Christmas carols in the cold. We swap desserts, celebrate birthdays, cook when someone is sick. Inge recently bought Big Wheel bikes for the neighborhood kids at a yard sale for when they stop by to visit our grandkids. We also prayed together when a neighbor's son was murdered, and another time when a wife was taken by ambulance to the hospital.

Our lives are infinitely richer through this experience of incarnational living in community. Christian living is so much more than going to church, we often say. It has only taken me about forty years to learn that.

Transitions

"It takes courage to grow up and become who you really are."
e. e. cummings

Sometimes the most difficult challenge for someone who feels the call of God to pursue urban ministry is to escape the gravitational pull of their theological upbringing and church background.

At least for many white Christians who have grown up in fundamental, conservative circles, the theological context in which they have been nurtured has not only been one with a strong evangelistic fervor and emphasis on Jesus, but also a corresponding, strong *resistance* to holistic ministry that does not see race, poverty, immigration and other social issues as legitimate ministry concerns. Couched negatively as the "social gospel," those concerns have been set in opposition to the gospel of Jesus. The assumption is, if your emphasis is sufficiently evangelistic and Jesus-focused you will refuse to be distracted by social issues.

Those who have been raised in such circles but who now have had their worldview and theology expanded and deepened, find that they don't fit in the old structures in which they were raised. Much like Elijah after the prophets of Baal experience, they feel isolated and alone. No one else has your concerns, God. I alone am left.

It is often traumatic and extremely painful for that person to strike out on a different trajectory. It is often disruptive to families. Family members, especially parents, feel it is a deep betrayal and a rejection of their faith. They feel this is a giant step toward the slippery slope of "liberalism," and so therefore marshal all of their influence and power to disrupt and resist.

For those who find themselves swimming against that current, I usually offer two thoughts:

First, be patient. Don't be too quick to throw overboard the training and church experience of your past. Careful. Are you just running away from something, or are you running to something?

The value of much of that will become clearer over time. Perhaps you will not take everything from your youth or past church experience, just as your parents probably didn't take everything from theirs, but you can take what was valuable and build on it. You don't have to burn the house down on your way out.

Second, for those who make major shifts; Catholic to Evangelical, Fundamental Baptist to Episcopal, etc, my advice is to go slow. Bring those you love along in your thinking and reasoning.

This is especially true when moving from suburban, mono-cultural ministry to urban, multi-ethnic ministry. Are you able to trace God's heart for the poor throughout Scripture, why he is so concerned about the immigrant and sojourner in the land, and show where God has a deep concern for justice for those on the margins? You should. Make your case biblically as well as personally. You won't shout others into accepting your position. In fact, you don't need to convert them to your point of view at all. You do want them to respect it, though, and you. Just be kind and firm.

I have often asked younger folks who are wrestling with parental acceptance of a new trajectory, "Didn't your parents raise you to trust Jesus and walk in obedience to him and the Bible? Isn't that what you are trying to do here? Use that to make your case with them. Help them to see that this is the outworking of their spiritual investment in you. You not only value it, you are trying to live as best you know how and follow the Spirit's leading. After all, you are not saying you have decided to sell drugs or are moving in with your boyfriend or girlfriend. You are trying to follow Jesus, and this is where he is leading."

Everybody has to trust God for new steps, you as well as those who love you. After all, it is a bit inconsistent for those who have carefully taught you to fly on your own and trust God as an adult, to say when you finally come to that point, "No, you shouldn't trust His leading, you should trust ours!"

Others have been here. You are not alone. Many have had to negotiate this minefield. It can be done.

Regardless of how difficult the transitioning into urban ministry is or how steep the climb is once you are immersed in it, it is worth it. William Carey, the father of modern missions once said, "If I had a thousand lives, I would give them all for India." I and many others throughout the urban communities of America would echo the same sentiment: "If I had a thousand lives, I would give them all for this neighborhood where you have planted me."

Living on the Edge

"And he trembling and astonished said,
Lord, what wilt thou have me to do?"
(Acts 9:6)

People often ask me if I know of sharp ministries or non-profits in the city that are really making a difference. They have a heart for people and need a summer internship or are graduating soon.

"But I'm looking for someplace that's hiring. I don't want to have to raise financial support," they quickly add. "That scares me to death. I could never do that."

"Oh, I don't blame you," I usually say. "I know exactly what you mean. You shouldn't do anything that scares you, or anything that may really push you out of your comfort zone. After all, you know the most important thing Jesus wants for you is to feel safe, comfortable and in control."

I try not to smile.

Eventually I respond to their puzzled looks. "Help me to understand," I venture. "You want to serve God and really make a difference with people on the margins, but you don't want to have to do anything scary? You want to help people launch out into new lives and levels of trusting God, but you don't want to sail beyond the security of your own safe little harbor in order to do that? How exactly would you radically call other people to live by faith, when controlling fear is in the driver's seat in your own life?"

I try to be gentle, but I keep nudging and poking them on that issue. You can see the wheels turning. I love the conversations that follow from that.

It really is fundamental. The starting point for determining what God wants to do in our lives can never be based on our *present* circumstances, resources or attainments. We can never stand and look at our greatest fears or lack of faith and make judgment calls concerning what we can or can't do.

The *first* question is paramount; Where does God want me? What does he want me to do? How will that happen, how will it be financed, who else is part of this vision, and when it should happen can only be answered after asking the "What" question.

Friends and Neighbors

"He who has friends must show himself friendly."
(Proverbs 18:24)

Inge has such a subtle, engaging, persuasive way about her with our neighbors. I marvel. She planted a "friendship tree" with Gloria, our next door neighbor yesterday. So sweet. Well, maybe. She practically dragged her introverted friend out of the house when she had balked at going shopping.

"Oh come on, Gloria, there's nobody going to see you! I'm going and look at me! Come on!" She finally relented. They had a blast, spent all their Black Friday money ahead of time, and came home with a carload of plants and trees. Both are gardeners, and they had such fun digging in the dirt and planting that stuff together. A strong German personality is handy sometimes with the reluctant.

As she waters the flowers she sees Hai, our Chinese neighbor. She waves, crosses the street, and for some reason is now in deep discussion with him about where the best alleys are to find scrap wood. He comes over to see her chicken coop in the backyard, built with all the free wood she has scavenged from dumpsters in the alleys.

Two weeks ago she took a birthday cake to Tony, a neighbor up the street, who was too shy or too preoccupied to come to our place for a birthday celebration. He joked early this morning as he walked his dogs past our house, "I'm blaming you for making me gain weight!" Laughter. Teasing. They paused for small talk with her about trash pickup and Daylight Savings Time. His wife is a schoolteacher. We have had several cookouts with them in the last two years, all because of Inge's winsomeness. She is irresistible. I might be a little biased.

Helen, our frail, 80 year old neighbor on the other side of us sticks a scrawled note in our door addressed to Inge: "Do you want to go to the museum with me?" Friends. They are such a hoot together, these two. Such sarcasm. They whisper and giggle like two schoolgirls. They conspire together and laugh about their husband's quirks; John's memory, my lack of gardening skills. Inge cooked for him a couple of months ago when Helen went to the hospital. Later Inge walks her home, slowing to her pace, holding her arm and an umbrella as they shuffle down the sidewalk as it begins to sprinkle.

Such a precious picture of friends and neighbors.

What Took You So Long?

"A story is the shortest distance between being a stranger and being a friend."
Paul Smith

Inge, ever the extrovert, met him several weeks ago. Our neighbor at the far end of the street had cut down a tree in his yard and since we have a wood stove, she asked him if we could have it.

Yesterday I finally stopped and introduced myself to make arrangements to pick it up, and you would have thought I was a long, lost relative. Roy had been waiting on me for weeks.

"Come in, come in!" he said as he swung open the screen door. "Your wife said you would come by. I wondered why it took you so long. Lydia, come out here and meet our neighbor!" I felt guilty I hadn't come earlier.

I learned his life story in 15 minutes. Eighty years old, he had been a B-29 pilot in Korea. "But I don't talk about it much," he said. "Not like those guys down at McDonald's." He belly-laughed.

He was sharp, witty and a little sarcastic, in a good way.

He worked for the post office for 54 years and married Lydia just four years ago. He opened his garage to show me his baby, a '66 Impala. I asked him if he drove it a lot.

"I've probably put 1,000 miles on it in the last ten years," he laughed.

He wore a crucifix around his neck. "So where do you go to church?" I ventured.

"Saint James. We got married in the church!" It was obviously important to him.

"We're followers of Jesus too," I said. I told him of Providence, and a bit of how I came to faith. We talked of the neighborhood, our military years, other neighbors. He has been here since the 1950's.

"Let me show you that wood," he said finally. We walked out back. "I grew up poor in Louisiana in the country cuttin' wood," he said as he pointed to it. "I sure ain't doing it now."

As I left he said, "Come back anytime except Tuesday evening. I go to Panera then to pick up their leftover bread and take it to the Denver Rescue Mission."

Roy is my kind of guy.

Who I Want to Be at 86

"Blessed is the society with elderly souls."
Lailah Gifta

I went to check on my elderly friend who lives on my street. You would think I was the president or the Pope the way he greets me and welcomes me. "Come in, come in!" he says as he unlocks the screen door. Would I like some tea? Something cold to drink?

Sitting at his dining room table, we talk. Or rather, he talks. I nod occasionally, just letting him ramble. When no one comes to visit very often, you have a lot of thoughts to get out.

Eventually I gently orchestrate my exit. When I am finally able to inch towards the door, he touches my shoulder. "Can we pray a little bit together?"

"Sure," I say, wishing I would have suggested it, pastor and all that I am.

We stand at the door with his hand on my shoulder as he prays first, and I feel like I'm in the presence of Jesus himself. It is surreal. Such compassion as he prays, such concern for people around the world; refugees, immigrants, poor, persecuted, war zones, the election, for this neighborhood, for me. I get choked up.

He is almost 90. This is who I want to be at his age. He thanks me profusely for stopping by. He's so grateful. So happy. He calls me a good man.

And he thinks I came to encourage him.

You Buy for Me, Yes?

"Be a star in someone's dark sky."
Matshona Dhilwayo

A woman in our church brought flowers to a couple with a newborn baby. Just as she left their house a taxi saw her and pulled to the side and the driver waved her over. She approached hesitantly since she hadn't flagged him.

"Please tell me," a young Muslim asked, placing his hand over his heart as an expression of courtesy and pointing to the house, "did they have baby yet?" His accent was thick; Arabic maybe, or Swahili.

"Yes, they did, last week in fact," she answered. A strange question from an unknown taxi driver, she had thought, but it was broad daylight and on a public street.

He gestured for her to wait, put it in park, and came around on the sidewalk. "Ah!" he said. "I want to honor them. He is friend. Can you help me?" He pulled out his wallet and thrust a $50 bill towards her. "Can you buy for me what will honor them? I don't know tradition here for new baby. You are friend too, no? Please! You help?"

She was startled, and brushed aside the money. "Oh no, it should come from you, not me!"

He held up both hands to show his helplessness. "But I don't know!" he said. "I want to honor. No offend. Please. I want to honor." She could see he was afraid of doing the wrong thing culturally.

For the next several minutes she talked to him about a baby gift, where to go to get a cake, what kind to get ("I told him not chocolate since she was probably nursing"), what to write on the cake and how to spell it. He seemed relieved as he wrote. "Good! Yes, good! Thank you. Thank you!" He placed his hand over his heart again to show his gratitude.

"I also told him that I was trying to befriend a Muslim family that just moved on our street, and that the man drove the same kind of taxi that he drove," she said. When I told him the street name his face lit up, called a name and said, "Ah, I know him! He is my friend, my buddy! Yes, my buddy! We drive! I tell him you help me!'"

She smiled and reflected on the sovereign hand of God who orders our steps. "I'm going to take that woman on our street flowers again this week and tell her how I met her friend."

Why I Don't Cut My Neighbor's Lawn

"Kindness is not in the things we say but in the things we do."
Abdulazeez Henry Musa

One of my neighbors is elderly and frail. He can't cut his grass any more. Not only do I cut my grass regularly, but I want to serve people in the name of Jesus. I want to offer to cut his grass for him. It would be easy for me, wouldn't take too long, he would be happy, and it would be a kindness and a great testimony of a "good neighbor doing good in the neighborhood."

Should I do it?

No.

Why? Shouldn't I take every opportunity to do good? Or am I just lazy? Self-centered? Don't care about people? Only concerned about my own stuff?

None of the above. Here is why I don't cut John's lawn.

Tony, 48 years old, my other neighbor, does lawn service and cuts it for him. It's likely the only work he can get. It's his income in the neighborhood. For me to do it for free as a good neighbor would undercut Tony, whose only means of income is cutting grass. In doing good to John, I would be hurting Tony. Imagine me now trying to talk to Tony about Jesus.

Such is the dilemma often for short term missions when they go to Haiti, or Mexico, Mali or somewhere else and want to do "free" construction or some other ministry for a church in the name of Jesus. Their hearts are in the right place. They want to help. They love Jesus and people. They have the manpower and the resources. But they do damage. They disrupt the local economy out of ignorance. Someone is out of work because those folks showed up.

"It is not good to have zeal without knowledge." (Proverbs 19).

It doesn't matter how excited you are to serve Jesus. If you are uninformed, you can hurt people with the best of intentions.

That's not an argument to stop helping people. It's an argument for learning to do it wisely.

Judge Tyrone

*"I don't become what I think I can,
I don't become what you think I can,
I become what I think you think I can."
Jawanza Kunjufu*

One of our staff members introduces a neighborhood kid to one of our staff members, an older African-American woman who has worked for decades with kids who are at-risk. He's ten years old.

"Sister Johnson, this is Tyrone Turner. (not his real name) He lives here in the neighborhood."

"How you doin' Tyrone?" she says.

She doesn't wait for a response. She comes from behind her desk, shakes his hand, cuts to the chase. "So what do you want to be when you grow up?"

Folks have been investing in him for a while.

"I would like to be a lawyer, or maybe even a judge," he replies proudly.

"Alright, alright. That's good. Real good. Glad to know you Judge Turner."

He wanders off, visits around the building. Meets other people. Shoots the breeze. Ends up back at her office. She looks up from her computer screen.

"Judge Turner! You have a good visit?"

"Yes ma'am."

"All right, Judge Turner. I'll see you again soon. Come back and see us!"

Such is the power of expectation.

Praying in the Front Yard

"One of the most important things you can do on this earth is to let people know they are not alone."
Shannon Alder

My neighbor John came to borrow a car seat for his great-grandchild. We had to wait for my daughter to bring it from her house, so we sat in the shade outside and talked.

My neighbor Kenneth, who lives next door on the other side, saw us and came to sit also. We were three old men shooting the breeze at 8:00 a.m.

John has seen it all. Raised in Mississippi, he speaks slowly, as only an elderly African-American man can, of lynchings and his interaction with whites over the years. It is brutal to hear. He spent 30 years in the military as a combat medic, defending the system.

Kenneth is slightly younger than me and also a veteran. He speaks in measured, thoughtful tones of countless stressful police stops and harassments. You can hear the anger, the pain in his voice.

Talk drifts to politics in this election season; the divisiveness, the hostility, the grief.

"People like me, it feels like we don't even belong here," he said.

I listened and lamented how deeply rooted race is as part of our collective lives and history. I reflected on what a gift it is to me to be friends with them, to live between and share life with two African-American men like John and Kenneth.

My daughter Abi arrived with a baby on one hip and a car seat on the other. We stood as she hugged them, made small talk and took the baby in the house.

"Can we pray?" Kenneth asked. He's a good man.

As we all prayed together there in my front yard for the brokenness and healing of our country, I got choked up. Such gifts of God, these men, friends sovereignly brought into my life to teach me and to give hope in the midst of discouraging times. They are both gifts and a reminder.

McDonald's at 7:00 a.m.

"Community is a sign that love is possible in a materialistic world where people so often either ignore or fight each other. It is a sign that we don't need a lot of money to be happy--in fact, the opposite."
Jean Vanier

There is something particularly endearing about all of the old men who gather at McDonald's early in the morning for coffee. Rushed people in business suits wait impatiently in line, multi-tasking on their phones. Bleary-eyed nurses in scrubs coming off of night shift slouch and check their order number again, waiting to be called, exhausted.

Not these gray-haired guys. These guys are out of the race. They have nothing else to do but shoot the breeze with their buddies. Those who still have wives have been 'shooshed' out of the house early. "Go! Do something!" they say.

I eavesdrop. Ex-Marines tease ex-Navy guys, and ex-G.I.'s mercilessly mock their ex-Air Force friends. It is a continual stream of corny jokes, laments about the weather, the chores that wait at home for them assigned by the wife.

Someone spills coffee and he shuffles to get the mop himself. "Get him a sippy cup!" "A straw!" the others shout. They flirt, innocently and grandpa-like, with the young girls in the Golden Arches hats. They all laugh and tease endlessly.

Eventually the group thins out; one by one they shuffle off towards home, or to get their oil changed, or drift over to the barber shop. They'll be back tomorrow for their senior coffee.

Why are they here? What is it that they are experiencing? It's relationship.

We are created for relationship as human beings. God exists in community as Father, Son and Holy Spirit, and we are created in his image. We long to be connected in meaningful ways with other human beings. It is universal. That is why solitary confinement is torture. It is not normal to be in isolation from others. The Church could perhaps learn something here; it may not be a doctrinal statement that creates an attractive community, it is the potential for meaningful relationship. Relationships are life.

At the Goodwill

"All I'm saying is, kindness don't have no boundaries."
Kathryn Stockett, The Help

Kindness is so winsome.

My wife Inge was at the Goodwill store last winter in a snowstorm. She told the older lady behind her in the checkout line, "Wait here, I'm taking my stuff to the car and I'll be right back to walk you to your car. It's very slick out." The lady was so grateful. They talked. Inge wrote down her cell number and gave it to her. She never heard from her again. That was six months ago.

Yesterday the woman called and explained she had lost Inge's number but just found it in her winter coat. "I was so happy!" she told her on the phone. "I just said to myself, I'm going to call right now!"

Inge invited her to tea this week. (And probably another Goodwill trip). "You were so kind to me that day at Goodwill," she said. "I've never forgotten it."

How normal it should be for Christians to be known for kindness and not simply our criticism of everything.

There is more to the story, however.

The day she called, Inge and I were in the midst of a home construction project. I had other things on my agenda, but she had hounded me enough that I relented. OK, I'll help. Now however, here we were, half-way done. She is on the phone talking as if she had all the time in the world, and I'm standing around, fidgety, anxious to finish.

I caught her eye and tapped my watch. "Come on," I mouthed silently. "Whoever it is, just tell her you'll call her back."

Inge sat down and nonchalantly continued a long, friendly conversation. I walked in front of her, tapped my watch again, a little more insistently. She ignored me, turned away and kept talking. When she finally hung up she told me who it was; the woman from the Goodwill six months before.

It was humbling. Why do I always think my issues are more important than everyone else's? I almost got in the way of something there, I thought to myself.

That experience was such a reflection of Inge's kind and winsome heart. When she walked that lady to her car in the snow she *could* have told her that the reason she was doing it was because she was a Christian, and did she know Jesus? She could have offered her a tract, standing there in the snow beside the car, with four propositional points on 'how to get saved.'

Instead, she offered her her cell phone number. She didn't simply offer her information, she offered her a relationship.

Loved and Wanted

"The first question which the priest and the Levite asked was: 'If I stop to help this man, what will happen to me?' But...the good Samaritan reversed the question: 'If I do not stop to help this man, what will happen to him?"
Martin Luther King Jr

The park was deserted tonight on this post-election nightly walk, except for one dark-skinned young couple that circled the one-mile loop around the lake opposite of me. As we approached each other in the dark I could hear their Arabic in the distance as they laughed, then it became hushed as they came closer. Under the streetlamp her eyes darted cautiously towards me. "Hello," she ventured softly as we made eye contact and passed. That's what you do to show you are not a threat. You speak, and feign a weak smile.

Another loop. She held his arm close as we passed, this time silently. She didn't look up.

I felt the Spirit prompting. If you see them again you should speak, he seemed to say.

We met for the third time on the other side of the lake. I slowed my pace a bit to ensure that we met under a streetlight. I didn't want to scare them; a white man, post-Trump election, at night, in the dark.

"Excuse me," I said, touching both hands to my chest so as not to be a threat. "Do you speak English?"

"Yes," she said cautiously. They slowed. She had to have wondered why I stopped.

I could hardly get it out, I was so choked up. "I just want to say, I am so sorry for Trump. This is not the America I know."

I was a total stranger, but their eyes softened, stances shifted. "Oh, yes," she said. "He is very disrespectful to people. Everybody." She spoke softly and respectfully of this one so hateful.

It was the beginning of a wonderful, endearing, gentle conversation with a young Ethiopian couple concerning the impact the election of Trump has had on their community. We stood there, strangers in the lamplight, separated by continents, culture and language, yet connecting as friends over the shared concern for the dignity of all human beings.

"We are all afraid," he said. "Are we going to lose our jobs, our everything? We talk a lot about such things." He had to search for some words. I teared up.

"I am so sorry. So sorry. I am 62 years old and this not us, this is not America," I repeated.

However naive it is, their hope is in the American system. "He is only one man," she said confidently. "He cannot do anything by himself." They have more confidence than I do.

"I don't want to hinder your walk," I eventually offered. "I just wanted you to know, that you are loved and wanted. God bless you."

"Thank you, thank you!" they said.

I fear for them, and for us as a nation.

Alone

"I fear being alone more than anything else. So why do I do this? Why do I push away the people I love? What is so very wrong with me? I don't know. And I don't know how to make it stop."
Victoria Aveyard

It was bitter cold and still snowing when the hearse pulled up. I was just a young college guy working as a cemetery groundskeeper.

Jerry the mortician got out, leaving the car and heater running. I had met him here often for funerals big and small, but this time it was only the hearse.

He pulled the scarf away from his face just enough for me to understand his muffled voice in the wind. "No one else is coming," he said. "It's just me."

"Just you?" I asked. I wondered about pall bearers.

He explained. An older homeless guy, probably drunk, walking in the bitter cold and snow had fallen and frozen to death in a ditch along the roadside. No family. No friends. No one at the end of a sad life.

He opened the back of the hearse. "It's just us two," he said, "but we can do it."

I had shoveled a path to the open grave through the snow, and we cautiously inched our way along with that heavy casket, two unknown workers carrying an unknown man to his grave. It was a long, heavy walk in the howling wind. We finally slid the casket onto the board, took time to catch our breath, and then turned the cranks that lowered him down. Jerry was anxious to get back to the hearse. I shoveled in the grave.

I have never forgotten the sadness I felt that day for a man I didn't know. Shovels full of dirt always sound so loud and jarring as they land on a casket lid. I wondered about his life; his childhood, high school years, who had loved him, whom he had loved. What were the storms that had driven his life against the rocks? Had he been a man of faith?

Usually there are flowers with a little color to leave behind and camouflage the ugly brown dirt and clods on the fresh grave, but not this time. The brown scar on the earth now was a sharp contrast to the white blanket across the cemetery. I picked up my pick and shovel, turned and walked back up the snowy path.

"So teach us to number our days." (Psalm 90)

II. FAMILY

Sunday Evenings

"We have all known the long loneliness, and we have learned that the only solution is love and that love comes with community."
Dorothy Day.

Community group last night was a room full of raucous, laughing, loud people. Kicking off their shoes at the door, they arrive sporadically and continuously pile into the family room, stopping only at the crock-pot to get a bowl of chili and other delights spread across the table. Everyone has brought something; drinks, desserts, both store-bought and home-made. The teapot is full. Some stand, others sit, regulars introduce themselves to the visitors and vice versa. Hugs all around. The glowing wood stove makes it cozy, more chairs are brought from other rooms.

As everyone eats, the buzz in the room slowly begins to wane. The decibel level drops eventually, and for the benefit of the visitors we go around the room getting to know each other. We shouldn't introduce ourselves, I say, but someone we know; a spouse, significant other, a friend. "Don't give us just resume stuff of that person," I caution. "Tell us something about them that helps us to know who they are, helps us to remember them." It's wonderful. It beats the hesitant, self-conscious, boring "I-don't-want-to-brag-on-myself" dance when we are left to introduce ourselves.

We brag on each other. Gush.

We spend time reading the Bible together. No one lectures; a number of folks around the room venture to share what they sense the Spirit is saying to them and us through the passage. Others follow suite. The voice of God sounds, incredibly, like Heidi. And Peter. And Nathan. And Megan. And Kristi.

Eventually we change gears and ask: How can we pray for you this week, specifically? Don't ask us to pray for your second cousin's friend's dentist appointment next week, we want to pray for you. How can we do that? We wait.

Hesitantly, a brother asks for prayer for his cancer treatment. We pause as a woman in the room who is a nurse in a cancer ward intercedes for him. She knows. She prays. We pray along with her, silently.

Another person asks for grace as there are layoffs tomorrow at his job and he needs grace and wisdom for whatever happens. A brother who has been there quickly volunteers to pray for him. He knows. He prays. We pray along with him silently too.

Someone else has a rare medical condition and is concerned about warm weather when it gets much worse. She's scared. A sister intercedes.

This is a praying bunch.

We stand and hold hands in a circle to finish. It's good to touch, to know another person is here, concerned about me, praying for me, praying for each other.

It occurs to me that a lot of stuff happens Sunday nights here. We eat. We have fun. Tease. Laugh. But if that is all we did, it wouldn't be enough. We really come to meet with God, and to hear from him, together, in community.

Afterwards they all hang around forever; in the living room, in the kitchen, on the lawn, leaning against their cars in the driveway. I can't get rid of them.

That's OK. I don't want to. They're family. And they are loved.

Overcoming Fear

"I don't trust anybody. Not anybody. And the more that I care about someone, the more sure I am they're going to get tired of me and take off."
Rainbow Rowell

It is a dance in the church foyer that is familiar to everyone.

"How are you?"
"Fine."
"How are you?"
"Fine."

Fine. Great. We're all fine.

Really?

A defining, controlling characteristic of human experience at the root of that dance in the church foyer? Fear.
...of being discovered as less-than.
...of never being loved.
...of not being accepted.
...of failing.
...of being inadequate.

That life-dominating and unbearable grip of fear can only be broken one place; in meaningful, significant, authentic, Spirit-soaked community.

It is there, in safety and acceptance, that broken people embrace each other's brokenness and speak life to each other in Jesus. It is in that place, in the light of love and truth, that the lies and irrational fears that play on loop in our heads and which keep us cowering and hiding in isolation are exposed. It is there in community that healing is found, courage is gained, confidence is found to be free and fully one's self as created by God.

To experience that depth of community is to recover an important function of the Body. It won't happen by yourself. It won't happen sitting in a pew or a standing in a church foyer. It will only happen in face-to-face authentic community with others.

That's not radical. That's Basic Christianity 101.

A Healing Community

Everybody says they want community until they experience it.

So many are "all-in" for the search for community, the search for the perfect community that will meet all of their needs; a place where they feel totally welcomed, loved, affirmed, challenged, heard, supported, nurtured, and embraced.

Such a community doesn't exist, but it can often be a consumeristic, self-centered dream. They are in essence searching for a unicorn, and when they fail to find that community which meets all of those idealized needs, they are disappointed, disillusioned, and quick to hit the ejection seat. "They just weren't meeting my needs," they will say.

That is a consumer mentality. Realistically, "community" means commitment to relationships that are life-giving but often less than ideal; it's living life with people that turns out sometimes to be messy, tedious and often exhausting. It means deep relationships with people who are very similar to you, somewhat different than you, and often radically different than you. It means life with people who are nurturing and funny, and others who are dark and draining, extroverts who talk too much and those who are paralyzed introverts; fundamentalists and liberals, people-pleasers and those who, if you bump them just a little, are incredibly angry beneath the surface with men, with women, with authority, with the church.

We all have issues. We all are broken, and we all need help. We all need Jesus, and we all need each other. God not only uses the Spirit, but our rough edges as sandpaper to file away the rough edges of each other's character.

It is tedious work.

On the other hand, it is the most life giving place to find yourself. For example, a great CG discussion last night around I John and the whole issue of forgiveness for believers.

So many of us, we discovered, have been steeped at some point in an environment where God was perceived simply as our greatest and constant critic, the harping "God of 100%." Arms crossed, glaring, huffy and tight-lipped because of our endless failures, God has often seemed to be a father who was always disappointed with us, saddened and ashamed that we never measured up.

When we eventually skulked back into his presence to ask forgiveness, (again), we felt such shame. "Really?" we would imagine him saying. "You're back here again? Haven't you confessed this a thousand times before? What is the matter with you? You are SUCH a failure."

John's words are freeing, a powerful antidote to toxic thinking. Jesus is not the God of shame and guilt. He is not our greatest critic but our greatest champion, our strongest advocate, our most loving, supportive, friend and father. He knows you, and you are loved. Lavishly. Intensely. Completely, not in spite of who you are, but because of who you are. When we grasp that, we no longer live out of shame for our sin, but live out of love because we are loved. It makes all the difference.

It was a life-giving discussion. Once you have experienced authentic community, you can never go back to just sitting through a service and calling that "church".

Grieving in Community

It's okay to be discouraged. It's not okay to quit.

Grief washed over me unexpectedly this week. Thirty-year old grief.

The wife of a couple in our church has been in the hospital for the last two months because of a difficult pregnancy. Complications had placed the baby at high risk, and the prognosis was not good. Only given a 5% chance of surviving birth, we all prayed for the best but prepared for the worst. For two months the church prayed, took meals to those at home, baby-sat and helped out while mom was hospitalized.

Last week, incredibly, baby Hannah was born healthy. Everyone was elated! Twitter and Facebook lit up with the news. I felt like Rhoda in Acts when the church was praying for Peter's release from prison, but then was surprised when the knock at the door was him.

The joy was short lived. Within 24 hours it was clear she had some serious internal problems, and emergency surgery was scheduled. Long, tense hours later the surgeons were grim; the parents should spend Hannah's last few hours with her; she would not survive.

Ah, such grief.

It was early on the morning of the funeral that I was on the bike at the gym and was overcome with grief myself.

Unexpectedly, I was transported back in my mind to August, 1984. Memories that had blurred around the edges over the years became incredibly vivid, memories of events that seemed suddenly as if they had just happened.

It was thirty years ago that my wife and I also lost a daughter at birth, a daughter that we named Hannah.

Those also had been long and difficult months. We had two children at the time, both under four years old, and Inge also had suffered through a very difficult pregnancy. As long months of bed rest dragged on we also had prayed with our church family, also had prayed for the best but prepared for the worst.

Months of scares, numerous false alarms, and multiple trips to the emergency room had worn us out emotionally and spiritually. One night in August when we made a trip to the ER they admitted her.

It was a long night.

Hannah died at birth. We held her there in the delivery room, wrapped in a tiny white blanket as her few minutes of life on this earth slipped away. The nurse cried. We cried. We prayed there in the delivery room over that little girl, for her and for us, holding both onto her and God and his sovereign purpose. He sustained us, but those were difficult times.

Emotionally numb, we went home the following day to an empty nursery. Inge packed away the newborn layette. We kept that bedroom door closed. The crib with the zoo animal mobile over it was too painful a reminder that Hannah would not be coming home.

Those were the memories that became so vivid to me that morning on the bike. I recalled the visits from friends and family; some to bring food, some to bring hugs and expressions of love, and those who came just to sit with us, silently, and mourn.

Looking back now the loss has far more depth, more texture. From this vantage point we now know what we lost with Hannah; first words, first steps, Christmas mornings, Sunday school, bike rides, beaches, homework and field trips, late night talks, boys, graduations, jobs, dreams, marriage, babies.

Life. We have missed life with Hannah.

Two days ago I was struck by what a friend remarked in passing; before too long we will see Hannah in heaven, running and laughing! He said it with such anticipation. For the last thirty years Inge has said, in times of tender reflection on those days, that perhaps our Hannah will be the one laughing, running to greet us, take us by the hand, and show us around heaven when we get there. Now I think maybe the Hannahs will be together.

Such losses may be how God gently pries our fingers, one at a time, off of this life that we so desperately hold onto now in order to prepare us for our own departure. We have so many to see on the other side, we fear the trip less and anticipate it more.

Hannah Ruth Cook 1984
Hannah Jane Ngatia 2014

The Swing of the Pendulum

"It's ironic that much material on spiritual growth has to do with practices, but when you ask people what has most shaped them, the primary response is the name of a person."
John Ortberg

Those who have been around church life any length of time know that theological positions and practice often swing like a pendulum from one extreme to the other within and across generations. Worship swings from liturgical to free-form and then back again, structure oscillates from house-church to mega-church and back again, lifestyle expectations alternate between strict legalism to antinomianism and back.

Every generation must face issues of balance, both theological and philosophical, and wrestle continually with renewal and the correction of extremes while being careful not to overcorrect. It is not easy to navigate such terrain.

In my opinion, the pendulum has swung alternately in this generation between commitment to Scripture and commitment to community. Although both are equally valid and critical to spiritual formation, the Church has tended to champion either the knowledge of Scripture at the expense of deep relationships, or spotlighted and encouraged deep community at the expense of deep knowledge of the Scriptures. You can fall in a ditch on either side of the road.

I came to faith a generation ago among conservative fundamentalists who were still in knee-jerk reaction mode to "the liberals." During the 1930's, mainline denominations had gradually lost their grip on a high view of Scriptures and its authority, and the conservative fundamentalist movement arose in opposition to them with a strong commitment to a literal understanding of the biblical text. Since that time a deep rift has separated these two theological camps and American Christianity.

In a desperate attempt to recover the authority of Scripture in the Church, conservative fundamentalists staked out as paramount a stance that emphasized primarily the teaching and preaching of an inerrant, inspired text of Scripture. Practically speaking, that meant that the Sunday school hour, Sunday morning worship, Sunday evening services as well Wednesday evening church services were preaching services, primarily concerned with verse-by-verse exegetical teaching of the text. Such preaching was the central theme not only of church, but of special seminars and conferences as well. Christian publishers spotlighted blockbuster best sellers, like *Battle for the Bible*, in every Christian bookstore. Fighting fundamentalists, as they came to be known, had all of these on their coffee tables and nightstands. They were defending the faith from the liberals.

That was the camp in which I came to faith. I was saturated in that position in my formal training, and argued that position for years. Almost all of us trained in that era made a point to put in our bulletins and on our church signs the phrase "A Bible-Preaching Church."

Unfortunately, every good effort can go to seed when pushed to the extreme, and after a while careful thinkers discovered that what was often lost among the faithful was a significant commitment to relationship. Churches were known for their high-power preaching ministries and well-taught congregations, but there were a lot of profoundly lonely, isolated, unconnected, hurting, disenfranchised people sitting in churches - who also just happened to know a lot about the Bible. These were people who could argue various rapture and eschatological views, who knew how to argue for the inspiration and inerrancy of Scripture and could lead an evangelism seminar, but didn't know the people in the pew next to them or their neighbors who lived on their street. What a price we paid to champion biblical knowledge at the expense of relationships and community.

As is often the case with extremes, the pendulum a decade or more ago began to swing back in the opposite direction. Churches began to reemphasize the value of relationships. Small group ministries and house churches were no longer novelties. People moved away from the infatuation with mega-churches and returned to the value of authentic relationships in small groups and house churches, which once again were seen as indispensable to spiritual growth and health. At the same time there was a lesser emphasis on Bible content. The pendulum has continued to swing. Now many ask the question, have we overcorrected? Henri Nouwen observed,

When we honestly ask ourselves which persons in our lives mean the most to us, we often find that that it is those who, instead of giving advice, solutions, or cures, have chosen rather to share our pain and touch our wounds with a warm and tender hand. - Henri Nouwen

Those alert to trends realize that there has been a cost. In the pursuit of close relationships and small group dynamics, the formal Sunday school hour in the average church has eliminated 50 hours per year of biblical education, and the elimination of the Sunday evening service has eliminated another 50 hours of biblical education per year.

Churches now must rely on a thirty-minute Sunday morning message and small groups meetings for doctrinal teaching, yet with many of those groups the format is much more about relationships and sharing life than the systematic teaching of Scripture. Survey pastors today and they will tell you on the one hand that people today are much more deeply committed to authentic relationships and community, but on the other hand know much less about the Bible and its authority. There has been a significant, verifiable erosion of a shared, deep common pool of biblical knowledge that informs the Christian life.

That is a troubling trend. Both relational community as well as biblical knowledge are needed in the church, but the present swing of the pendulum is producing a generation of biblically illiterate Christians.

Promptings

Dear Jesus, do something.
Vldimir Nbokov, Pale Fire

On a walk two nights ago I felt an unusual, sudden pressing need to pray for a friend that I knew was facing a tough circumstance the next day. After I had spent some time doing that, I thought to myself that I should text him and tell him that I had felt suddenly this urge to pray for him.

I didn't. I wondered what he would think of me.

The next afternoon I saw him and he was elated. He had just experienced a major breakthrough in his circumstance that morning.

I have been reflecting since then why I was reluctant to text him the night before.

I think it was because I am still in recovery from a background that taught that any subjective experiences or feelings connected with God are suspect, and that God only communicates through Scripture.

How strange. Actually it would be odd if a personal God with whom we are in a personal relationship *didn't* communicate personally about specific issues.

The impulse to pray specifically for him was legitimate, and I should have encouraged him by letting him know.

I'm still learning. And unlearning.

A Theology of Hanging Out

"Where are you staying?"
the disciples to Jesus

When the disciples were intrigued and drawn to Jesus, their first question was "Where are you staying?"

It was a relational question. They wanted to hang out. They didn't want to just know more of his theology, there was something about his life they wanted to experience.

It is interesting to consider what they didn't ask:

Time and date of his next seminar

Location of those sessions

The topics of his future sessions

If he was published

If he had a complete doctrinal statement in print they could review prior to the next session

Where he went to seminary and what degrees he had

It is an issue worth considering. Does information trump relationship? Is it possible in our day that the role of significant life relationship has been minimized, perhaps even superseded, by an over-emphasis on theological information-transfer in formal classroom and teaching settings?

Mostly the latter was how I was trained. Mostly the latter is how I have trained others, unfortunately.

Not all such classroom contexts are counter-productive. It can often foster, however, a primarily 'informational' stance towards discipleship and maturity, where both tend to be measured by the amount of data acquired. In such a world, spiritual growth equals more information acquired.

That may not be the best yardstick by which to measure. Jesus might have been on to something with his model of relational discipleship.

Cleaning Up a Mess

"Forgiveness. Can you imagine?"
Lyrics from It's Quiet Uptown, Alexander Hamilton

No doubt I have often resisted the promptings of the Spirit to go back and clean up some relational mess. This time I didn't.

I wrote a long letter early this morning detailing my regret over a note I had written years ago to a pastor friend and his wife over some perceived injustice towards me. I had been hot under the collar at the time and wrote a sharp letter to let them know clearly and forcefully how wrong they had been. It could have been a legal brief; tightly reasoned, strong language, compelling argument.

It turned out to be a misunderstanding. We subsequently worked through it, but now lately, years later, I have not been able to escape the Spirit's conviction that I had not resolved that well. I had used my ability to write as a weapon. I decided yesterday to backtrack and clean up the mess.

It was a painful letter to write, not because I was reluctant to confess my wrongdoing. I was anxious to do that. The pain I felt was because I had to revisit the deep hurt I had intentionally caused friends whom I had known and ministered with for years.

They could have minimized my concern, side-stepped and responded with typical Christianese, "Oh, that's fine, don't worry about it. No big deal."

They didn't. My friend took the time to write back the warmest, kindest, most affirming, life-giving letter detailing how painful it had been, yet how God has used that in his life at the time. He recounted how we all had learned something, graciously celebrated our friendship and how God has used our ministry together since that time in significant ways. It was a page-and-a-half, single-spaced letter of pure grace, love, kindness and maturity.

I'm still learning at 62.

Speaking Life

I can live six months on one good compliment.
Mark Twain

You can actually see the impact physically on a person's face, a person's countenance.

I saw it tonight, the powerful effect of public words of affirmation.

At the staff Christmas party, old-timers with the ministry were asked to stand, and the newbies invited to share the impact they have had on them. Then it was the newbies turn for the old-timers to affirm something positive they had seen in them.

It was amazing to watch. Really. Verbalized, authentic words of affirmation are so life-giving, so encouraging, such a powerful communication of someone's worth to others.

We all get our fair share of hostility and criticism. Others often have no qualms about unloading their frustrations or disappointment with us. It wears on us, exhausts us, defeats us.

But to know that we are valued and loved by others, to hear those words spoken out into the air, in public, in front of others? It does something to our spirits. It is priceless.

I see you. I value you. You mean something to me.

So speak up. Speak life. Make the effort. Tell someone what they mean to you. Specifically.

Awkward? That's OK. It's not about you. Practice until it's not.

The Sovereignty of God

It is a most blessed thing to be subject to the sovereignty of God.
John Calvin

I have always loved the fact that God supernaturally rearranged the entire population of Palestine to get Mary and Joseph to Bethlehem through the decree of Caesar Augustus.

God is sovereign.

This morning a dear Kenyan believer and shepherd among our refugee population here at Providence asked me where the African church that she also shepherds could find a drum set. "My people, you know, must have drums to worship," she said with a smile with her gentle and beautiful Swahili accent.

I actually had a drum set in my basement that I bought years ago used off of Craigslist for $400 that I rarely played. "I could sell you my set for what I paid for it," I offered. A new set would cost probably $2000.

She was ecstatic. "Four hundred?! We have collected already $150. Can I pay you the rest later?"

"Of course," I responded.

I took them over to their church that afternoon. The Swahili service had already started.

As I set it up for them in the background, I reveled in the enthusiastic worship of this small, beautiful church; singing, dancing, prayer. It was moving. A little bit of heaven. God prompted me as I watched and listened; "Jeff, just give them the drum set."

I leaned into the ear of my pastor friend and asked her if it would be OK if I just gave the set to the church. I didn't want to be offensive, so wanted to check first. Her face lit up, and she shared that desire with the congregation. This poor, refugee church of Africans erupted in praise, and many came to hug me and thank me. I was embarrassed. We did only what we ought to have done.

If you think I wrote this post to highlight my generosity, you are mistaken. I actually write it in awe of the sovereign hand of God. In hindsight, here is what led up to that happening. I learned this all afterwards.

This tiny church had been borrowing the drum set from the larger church with whom they share a building, but the drummer told them they couldn't use it anymore.

They prayed last week and asked God for a drum set. They collected a grand total of $150 and then searched Craigslist, but could find nothing in that price-range. Drums might as well have been 4 million dollars. They were very discouraged.

God sovereignly arranged details. The pastor had the conversation with me this morning about drums, God poked me, and now this afternoon they are worshipping with a drum set that had been collecting dust in my basement.

It was a powerful reminder to all of us that God is good, sovereign, and that he will orchestrate the details to accomplish what is best for us.

God's Protection

All for one and one for all, united we stand divided we fall.
Alexandre Dumas, The Three Musketeers

Last night in our community group we were reading John 17 together and the Spirit turned up the volume on verse 11 for all of us. "Protect them Father," Jesus prays, "so that they may be one, as we are one."

It was as gradual as a sunrise, but with growing clarity we heard what was being said. We discovered, upon deeper reflection, that the protection Jesus prayed for is not praying that each of us individually would be protected from sickness, or pain, or disappointment, persecution or financial difficulties. Rather, he was praying that we, collectively, would be protected from division. He is praying for unity.

That truth dropped heavy in the center of the room because most of us have come from fundamentalist contexts where separating for the most minute reason is what you did to defend truth. If you didn't separate from someone who was doing something unacceptable, you separated from someone who was friends with someone who was doing something unacceptable Second degree separation. The circle gets smaller and smaller until we are the only ones left.

If unity among his followers is the primary concern of Jesus for his people on his deathbed, *where should we expect Satan's primary focus of attack to be? Where should we expect the most difficulties to come in a group of Jesus followers?*

Research the data on church splits and you will find few churches split over doctrinal issues, they split over personal or relational issues.

Satan gets his greatest mileage over division in the church brought on by personal issues and preferences.

We would do well to teach and preach this. When there are difficulties, maybe the first order of business is to reaffirm our commitment and unity and to remind ourselves that Satan desires to cause disunity at any given point.

From my army days I recall that the first step in defining a battle plan is to define the threat of the enemy.

We should be aware that an issue is never just an issue. It is a wedge that Satan desires to use to separate God's people.

Divide and conquer.

Learning Curve

No part of the Body has the right to say, I have no need of you.
(I Corinthians 12:20-21)

If you were to ask many middle-class, conservative white Christians to rate themselves on their understanding of urban issues such as poverty, race, class, and social justice issues, they will usually rate their understanding as fairly low on the following awareness scale:

Not at all aware → slightly aware → moderately aware → very aware → extremely aware

Some will vastly overrate their competence, and others will be fairly humble, self-aware of their own limitations, and recognize that their backgrounds have given them perhaps limited exposure to such issues.

Let any of them, however, immerse themselves in a class or ministry where those issues become front and center, and something happens! Having taught urban ministry for over twenty years at the university level, I have come to recognize an almost universal phenomenon as people actually become more aware, informed and engaged relationally and emotionally with people immersed in these contexts. The more personally engaged they become with folks facing these issues and the more aware they become of the challenges people face outside of the middle class, *the more often they tend to demonize their own social class, first cautiously and then more vocally.*

I can look back at my own journey into urban ministry and see the same phenomenon. It is a distorted way to manage the frustration and powerlessness people now feel about a reality they have not known before. There is often a deep embarrassment over their former lack of awareness and materialistic former selves, as well as a deep identification with and concern for real people they now know facing these issues. As a way to regain a bit of equilibrium in their thinking, they tend to blame-shift by demonizing the rich and making them their primary targets of criticism. Everyone gets painted with the same brush. Every wealthy person becomes a faceless, generic Wall Street "fat cat," selfish, self-consumed and mocked for their "lack of concern for the poor."

That is not true and it is not fair.

Of course, many rich *may* be oblivious and unconcerned about those farther down the economic strata. They *may* be driven by greed or self-interest. Anyone who lived through the 2008 crash of Wall Street knows that is true.

My experience is, however, that many, many wealthy Christians are acutely aware of their position, and genuinely desire to steward their resources to help and invest in others in in significant, meaningful, and empowering ways. I have seen it in every urban ministry of which I have been a part and have been deeply grateful for their example and investment.

It is unfair and unchristian to paint every wealthy person with a broad brush of self-centeredness and lack of concern for God's agenda. We all bring something to the kingdom table unique to us. Welcome. May Jesus be honored as we serve together.

III. LOVED AND WANTED

William on Colfax

You can't fix everybody. But there is no one you cannot love.

We met early Sunday morning, probably 5:00 a .m. when I answered the incessant pounding on the door of the ministry center. It was 40 degrees, he was in a short sleeve T- shirt, shorts, shivering to the point of almost convulsing.

"Can I come in and just get warmed up?" he asked. "Just to use the bathroom?"

I hesitated, made a judgment call and let him in. I was alone. I immediately regretted it.

He talked incessantly. He was Jesus, although people didn't recognize him. He had won 40 million dollars in the lottery but the IRS was stealing it from him. He was just waiting on a check from another source, and he was going to go down to the Readyman day labor place and give everybody who didn't get out that day $500. That's just the kind of guy he was. He was a king; he had a solid gold toothbrush worth a million dollars that someone had stolen from him. A machine-gun talker. He never caught his breath.

We sat and talked. Or rather, he talked. I plotted my escape route to the front door. I feigned interest and tried to figure out my next move.

Some people who hated him were trying to kill him in the spirit realm, but he wasn't going to press charges. Whatever that meant.

He rattled on. Gradually I felt less threatened. My heart warmed towards this sad guy, William, who had wandered in off of the street. I began to see and hear him differently; as someone's son. My son. Someone's needy, sick, lonely brother. Someone loved at some point by someone, now so alone and on the street in 40 degree weather in a t-shirt. As he shook and droned on, I remembered my psych nurse daughter saying that one of her greatest assets in helping people with mental illnesses was to develop rapport. People feel valued and dignified when you treat them with respect, when you dialogue with them as human beings, broken as they may be.

My heart softened as we sat on those uncomfortable folding chairs. I looked him in the eye. I nodded. I began to picture him as the man in the tombs who was possessed; a sad, tormented person in pain with nowhere to run. Voices he couldn't escape, life spinning out of control, out of touch with reality.

Eventually a worker from the ministry center appeared to vacuum the auditorium. I breathed a little easier.

"Do you think we could turn that coffee pot on?" he asked. His voice still shook from the cold. "Can I help you set up these chairs? Would you have another pair of pants I could have? A shirt? That guy at Readyman stole my check. Its Sunday, I haven't been able to get something else. That 40 million dollar check should come soon. Then I'll be all right."

Ah, William.

I can't fix him. He will stay here through the church service, they will feed him and be kind to him. Talk with him. Let him talk. Get him coffee. Then he will wander off down Colfax Avenue. A lost soul, voices in his head, talking of kings and golden tooth brushes and 40 million dollar checks.

Words imprinted on my mind years ago by someone more street-wise than I surface: "You can't fix everybody. But there is no one that you cannot love."

Some, like William, are probably not going to get fixed this side of heaven. Even if/when he comes to faith, his circumstances are not going to change much. He is too far gone. He's probably not going to become a good spouse, father, responsible employee, home owner or elder material. He may. But miracles are called miracles for a reason. They are not the norm.

He is still worth loving.

If you have a William that you love out there somewhere tonight; just know, God in his tenderness and goodness knows and sees them. And loves them. They are not alone.

Welcome Home

Only those sick with the shame and smell of a self-made pigsty in a far country know the deep meaning of these words: 'Welcome home my son. Welcome home'.

We adopted a rescue dog this afternoon. Annabelle, a Maltese mix.

My street cred is shot, of course. Any self-respecting Rottweiler or Pit would eat this thing as a snack. Eight pounds and a sweater. I'm so embarrassed. The things we do for love.

Inge and my daughter Natalie wanted to go to the shelter this afternoon and "just look." Ha! Really? Two rescuers should walk through those kennels and not rescue something? Not a chance. I knew that soon we would have a dog sleeping between us.

Little Annabelle already is making the wheels turn in my head. When we saw her in that place she had no hope. In fact, if no one adopted her she would have been destroyed. Running away from the care of her owner, she ran her right into the worst possible situation. The first flush of freedom as she bolted must have faded quickly as she found herself on her own; shivering in the snow, ripping open garbage bags for food, lonely and terrified. Everything is a threat 'out there' when you are eight pounds. And now, here she was. Caged, clock ticking towards her end.

We chose her and took her home. Paid to do it. Love her already! Delight in her, enjoy her, revel in the richness already that she adds to our lives!

We didn't do it because she was worth it, because she's not exactly a fine specimen. Matted, still grubby, needs medical care. Wheezes.

Limps on a back leg. She's not a hunting dog that has something to offer us. Not a show dog that can earn her way. She doesn't even do tricks. We adopted her, love her, brought her home and into our lives because we want her there. She is worth loving. That's all. She doesn't understand it, and no doubt couldn't explain it. But she doesn't need to. She's with us.

I stare at her now at home; warm, fed, loved, cared for, light years from where she was out there on her own, and I realize I am looking at myself, my life.

I was a stray. Bolted to freedom and misery.

I too am home now though, because God went and brought me home. I can't explain that either. But I don't have to. I'm with him.

Thanks for Talking to Us

"A litany of headlights blinding her
she stands unsteady on the dotted line,
takes timid steps towards rolled up windows
behind which any horror could crouch…"
Betriz Fernandez

I spotted a shopping cart and a bicycle on my nightly walk in City Park, pushed up under the overhang of the pavilion. As I got closer I could see someone in a sleeping bag, sitting up against the wall. I paused, maybe 30 yards away. "You doin' alright?"

"As best as could be expected," a voice answered. It was a woman's voice. I approached slowly so I wouldn't scare her.

"Happy Holidays," she said. It was only 9:00 p.m. Half-way sitting up in a sleeping bag, big Russian hat and mittens, she was at least 50. It was obviously going to be a long night, low 30's were predicted.

"The police aren't harassing you?" I marveled. She was in a brightly lit spot, no doubt for safety. But it made her more visible to the police. It made me wonder.

"The Rangers said they wouldn't bother us," she responded. A deeper voice then said, "He didn't invite us to move in here, but they said they would leave us alone." Ah, someone else was here too. Someone was in that pile of stuff next to the cart, a man. That was good. At least she wasn't out here alone.

"I saw they were sweeping people off of the street down on Park Street next to the Mission," I ventured, trying to make conversation. "You come from there?"

"We're not street people," she said, "not like some of those folks down there. They all get drunk down there. We are trying to get off the street. We hope to be off by the first of the month."

We made small talk. Talked of the cold, the fact that the Rangers wouldn't harass them, praise God, and their hope to get off the street.

It's always my dilemma. You can't fix everyone, but there is no one you can't treat with dignity and show the love of God.

"Stay safe," I said eventually as I turned to go. "God bless you. Nice to talk to you."

"Thanks for speaking to us," they both said from inside their sleeping bags. "God bless you. Have a good Thanksgiving."

I turned the corner and thought of how long the night was going to be for them. I paused, checked my wallet. Five singles.

I went back. "I wish I carried more cash," I said. "It's only five bucks. It might get some breakfast though."

"God bless you. Thank you. Every bit helps. Thanks for speaking to us."

I walked further around the lake, back to my car.

And wept.

Community

"There is no significant change without significant relationship."

Many of us in conservative circles have had drilled into our thinking that a widespread and indiscriminate 'telling' of the facts of the gospel is the essence of evangelism. On occasion we hear a gripping testimony of someone converted during a conversation in an airplane, or a chance encounter with a waitress that led to her conversion right at the table. People nod in agreement. The power of the gospel.

Privately though, if pressed, many wonder. They often feel unspiritual and guilty to verbalize it, but in a safe context they will confess hesitantly that they are uneasy with how few enduring results they have ever seen from such drive-by methodology. Professions? Sure. The problem is, what to do with the common knowledge that so many 'professions of faith' endure only about as long as the conversation? We all know people who have prayed a prayer, walked an aisle or said "yes" to Jesus on a street corner, but have shown no evidence of life or conversion.

"Oh yeah, I've been saved," an unsteady guy with glazed eyes and slurred speech told me once. "I've been saved a couple of times."

There may be a reason people often doubt the power of the gospel to actually change people. We have isolated the communication of facts about Jesus from the context of a supportive community and relationships. We have distilled conversion into an intellectual affirmation of facts about Jesus, when in reality it is much more; an entrance into a totally different life and world, an unfamiliar new world where one needs accompaniment, companionship, and direction from both Jesus and others.

It is not the power of the gospel to change lives and destinies that is lacking. What is often lacking is an understanding of the importance God places on the role of community and relationship in Christian conversion and growth.

We're All Broken

"I thank you, Lord, that I am not like other people… or even like this tax collector."
(Luke 18:11)

If you talk regularly with homeless folks, you know that some of the people with the deepest faith in Jesus slept out on the street last night, somewhere.

They might not fit the middle-class mold of what a "good Christian" is. They might not be able to defend a precise, 10 point doctrinal statement, or discuss four major eschatological positions, or compare and contrast Calvinism and Arminianism. But they know Jesus. They trust him, desperately, at the core of their being.

I'm not talking about people who feign faith in order to get something, who know how to manipulate in order to survive. Plenty have learned how to play that game.

I'm talking about people who know him, rest in him, trust him, who live in the moment, who cry out to God daily, and yet also get high or drunk to dull the pain. Folks who can't hold a job, have anger management issues, are depressed, hear voices, and alienate everyone around them.

They have issues. But on the other hand, so do you, so do I. Ours are just a bit more socially acceptable, deemed more worthy to be overlooked, minimized, excused, or tolerated.

Oh God. We are all broken. We all need Jesus. Help.

Lord, be merciful to me a sinner. (Luke 18:13)

First You Have to See

When he saw the crowds, he had compassion on them.
(Matthew 9:36)

A house was repossessed across the street from us, the people were evicted, and it was an eyesore. Whoever owns it eventually hired some day-laborers to clean out the house and clean up the property. It turned out to be truckloads of debris, brush and trash. Inge, ever the concerned mom and neighbor, went to see them as the young men worked outside.

"Are you guys staying hydrated?" she asked. It's always a question in the summer in Denver with its high altitude, dry blazing heat and cloudless skies.

"Can you believe that place sent them on this job and they don't even have a bottle of water?" she fumed. "And the water is turned off in the house!"

She came home and fixed them sandwiches and took them a pitcher of ice water.

"Juan and Derrick," she told me.

No Drive-By Ministry

"Seek the welfare of the city where I have sent you."
(Jeremiah 29:7)

Why is Matthew's version of the Great Commission so often considered more important than the other three gospels? Considering that all four gospels record their own version of it, it is a bit odd that Matthew's seems to trump all others in terms of familiarity with Christians.

We lose the richness of what God wants us to know when we pick and choose favorite passages and minimize others. Matthew gives us the *goal* which is to "make disciples" (Matt 28:19), but John gives the *methodology*: "As the Father has sent me, so send I you." (20:21)

How had the Father sent him? The methodology of Jesus for global evangelization is *incarnational presence*. "The Word became flesh and dwelt among us." (1:14)

That's more significant than we might think.

He could have done a quick drive-by from heaven and just made sure he was out of the neighborhood by dark. He didn't.

Instead, Jesus left his neighborhood and moved long-term into our neighborhood. He refused to let fear control him. He invested himself long term in a specific, ethnically identifiable, poor, oppressed community. He willingly entered into all of the blessings and challenges of that particular neighborhood; weddings and funerals, feasts, storms, and oppressive soldiers. He knew what it meant to live among religious bullies who exploited the vulnerable, he knew broken women, the homeless, the mentally ill as well as the occasional rich kid. He knew what it was like to live daily under the boot of Rome.

Jesus' focus in coming was not simply the transfer of theological data, to just verbally communicate propositional truth statements. Rather, he came, invested in a community, and gave them something much more valuable; he gave them himself. He gave his life to this community. The rhythms of their lives became his, the problems of their community became his. Their experiences, good and bad, public and private, political and personal, were his.

Our preoccupation with Matthew's goal of "making of disciples" may have produced in us the unintended consequence of prioritizing the transfer of information as our primary responsibility while simultaneously sidestepping the importance of incarnational, relational, physical, long-term presence, especially among the poor. It is no small issue.

"Witnessing" must be more than telling people things in airports, leaving tracts in restaurants, and boycotting Starbucks for their stance on gay marriage. To champion words to the exclusion of relationship and life is to truncate the gospel message.

Telling people spiritual facts in a poor, urban community while being unwilling to move into the neighborhood, settle down, raise families there and seek its welfare should give us pause, and indeed, drive us as followers of Jesus to rethink our paradigms.

Please Don't Give Me a Christian Cellmate

You don't bring healing to a broken world and broken community by volunteering an hour a week. It takes people who have signed their death certificates ahead of time and who lay down their lives every day, wherever they are, for a kingdom agenda.

Men filed in, 40 identical green-scrub prison uniforms. Black, White, Latino. Smiles, handshakes, man-hugs. Greetings all around. Most carried Bibles. Two guys on the guitar and keyboard fiddled with the instruments. Another guy on the front row sifted through a stack of acetate overheads, choosing songs. (Really!)

Mike-who-has-done-36-years-so-far got us started. Oh my. Lord I Lift Your Name on High, The Battle Belongs to the Lord. The songs were as outdated as the overhead projector. The guys on the instruments did their best, but struggled. Wrong chords, lost their place in the song. Tempo lagged. Overhead projector guy didn't keep up with the changing verses.

It was wonderful.

Really. No one snorted at the lack of "professionalism." No one rolled their eyes as the musicians struggled. No one huffed their dissatisfaction that they "just couldn't worship" in that atmosphere. We were in the midst of a couple of dozen felons who loved, worshipped and served Jesus in a Level IV maximum security prison. They were glad to be together for 90 minutes with their brothers in Christ. We were grateful to be there with them.

Inmates testified about the goodness of Jesus in their lives. Another inmate preached a message on glorifying God in prison, whether they will be paroled or not. They challenged each other to serious accountability. Later at a round-table discussion men talked of actually wanting a Christian cell-mate, but praying that God would give them a non-Christian because it would be a better opportunity to talk about Jesus.

No arrogance. No abrasiveness. No bible-thumping. Just an awareness that when a man is looking at decades in a maximum security prison, hope has to come from outside, from above. They know. They are there. And they want other men to know.

Humbling. Energizing. Deeply transforming. Maybe "remember those in prison" isn't just for the benefit of those on the inside.

Nowhere to Go

"Sometimes it's easy to walk by because we know we can't change someone's whole life in a single afternoon. But what we fail to realize it that simple kindness can go a long way toward encouraging someone who is stuck in a desolate place."
Mike Yankoski

She was Samoan or Hawaiian I think, dressed in a strikingly beautiful red, but clearly worn sari. She was probably 40 or 45 years old, although hard to tell. The years had not been kind to her. She appeared odd and a bit out of place in front of the Denver Rescue Mission today in such bright colors. Animated, loud, and argumentative, she was engaged in a spirited, emphatic, and often angry conversation with another person beside her.

Only there was no one there.

No one else paid any attention, snickered, or pointed. Surrounded by so many destitute here in front of the Mission, they simply ignored her ranting. Just one more person with an issue, working it out.

It's what you do when you can't afford a therapist, or have health care.

What do you do when you can't escape the voices in your head, and can't afford the medicine that will muffle them? How do you hold a job, keep an apartment, pay bills when they won't leave you alone, won't let you sleep, dominate your thoughts, torment you?

You don't, usually. Eventually if you don't have a safety net of family or friends you often end up here, in front of the Denver Rescue Mission, trying to get a bed or mat for the night, fallen from grace, arguing with no one and everyone.

Praise God for those who are deeply invested in loving, serving and walking with those loved by him, yet hold so little promise for significant change. If truth were known, she is probably never going to become a leader in some church. She won't be asked to head up some development committee or teach Sunday school.

Yet she is a precious daughter of God, created and loved by him.

Some of us will sail into heaven, as Ruth Bell Graham has written, "strong and under full sail." Others will wash up on that distant shore, broken and in pieces, gathered by Jesus who walks those shores looking for such.

Impossible

When Jesus saw him lying there and learned that he had been there a very long time, he asked him, "Do you want to get well?"
(John 5:6)

"Do you want to get well?" Jesus asked.

That is a strange question, Jesus. Why ask? The guy has been there on the same corner for 38 years, crippled, begging. Just go ahead and fix him.

Not so fast. If you have been around the block a few times in ministry, you know that not everyone is looking for a solution to their problems. Many are problem oriented and not solution oriented, content to simply lament their brokenness.

A problem, in fact, can become so much a part of a person's identity for so long that it becomes almost part of their DNA; it becomes who they are, at least in their eyes. They can't imagine who they are apart from it, or if things could ever really be different.

Sometimes it feels too risky, too painful, too scary to turn something loose. Uncomfortable? Yes. Unpleasant? Certainly. Painful? Without question. But here, in the middle of this ongoing mess, the pain is at least something familiar. To want to be different, to want to change, would mean they would have to discover who they are without it.

Life apart from cigarettes or weed? How would I even get through the morning, let alone the rest of my life? Goodbye to alcohol, forever? Unimaginable. Celibacy? You might as well ask me to give up breathing.

Do you want to get well, Jesus asks. Do you want things to be different? He is not going to drag anyone kicking and screaming into a new life. Nor can anyone else.

A healthy and workable philosophy of ministry is rooted in the example of Jesus. Those who desire to help should never work harder than the person who needs help. The response must be proportionate. Those who want to get well, those who are desperate enough to want to be delivered regardless of what it takes, will find him.

I'll Find My Way

The thief runs when no one is chasing him.
(Proverbs 28:1)

Ring

"I am so lost."
"Really? I gave you the instructions for how to get here."
"I know, but I thought I knew the way."

"It's OK. Use your GPS. It will show you the way."
"Alright. I will. I'll find it. See you soon."

Ring

"I am still so lost."
"Really? Did you follow your GPS?"
"Well, no."
"Why not?"
"I just thought I could figure it out."
"Well, that's where feelings will get you. Follow your GPS. It will tell you where to go."
"OK. You're right. I know that. I should have done that to begin with. Thanks for the reminder. You're the best. I'll do that now. Be there soon."

Ring

"Ugh. I am still so lost. I'm sorry. I need your help. Don't be mad."
"I'm not mad. Did you follow your GPS?"
"No, actually I just got to thinking that I have tried it in the past, but you know sometimes that thing doesn't work right."
"Really? Did you try it?"
"No, but I know it doesn't work sometimes. You know?"
"Let me check where you are. (checks GPS) You are on the wrong road. Take the next exit, turn around come back."
"Are you sure? The way I'm going seems like the right direction. I don't think I'm that far off."
"You are on the wrong road."
"Oh, OK. OK. Ugh. You're right. I know you're right. Thanks. See you soon."

Ring

"Don't be mad. I am still so turned around."
"Did you get off on that exit, turn round and come back?"
"No."
"Why?"
"Well, I have already come so far on this road. I hated to think about

driving all that way back."

"But you are on the wrong road."

"I know, but I just thought if I kept driving in this direction I would probably find my own way back. I thought I could figure it out."

"You are on the wrong road"

(Pause) "Why are you always so judgmental? Haven't you ever taken a wrong road?"

"Yes. That's why I am telling you to get off, turn around and come back. You are on the wrong road."

(Defensive) "Well, a lot of other people have taken this road too, you know. It's not like I am the only one. Why do you always have to be right about everything?"

"I know other people have taken it. I've been on it myself. But it's the wrong road."

"OK, OK. So what do you want me to do?"

"Get off, turn around and come back."

(deep sigh) "OK. You're right. I will. Thanks for speaking truth to me. I know you are always in my corner. I'll be there soon."

Ring

"Alright. I know what you are going to say so don't say it. Don't be mad. And don't lecture me. I don't need that right now. I'm still on the wrong road."

"Did you get off where the GPS told you, turn around, and come back?"

"No. I know what you said, but I got to talking to my friend and she convinced me she knew where I was and knew a better way to get back."

"But are you still lost?"

"Well, yes."

"Do you see a pattern here?"

(Angry) "Why do you have to be so judgmental?"

"I'm not being judgmental. It's just that you are on the wrong road, I and the GPS are both telling you that you are on the wrong road *and* how to get back, but you have a thousand reasons why you haven't actually done it and made it home. Haven't we had this conversation before?"

(sigh) "I am such a screw-up."

"Stop. You are not a screw-up, you are just on the wrong road. Other people have been there, me included. Get off, turn around, and follow your GPS back here where you ought to be. The wood stove is toasty, the table is set, everyone here is beyond excited and waiting for you to get here. We're waiting and we love you!"

"WHY ARE YOU ALWAYS SO CRITICAL OF ME?"

click

Full Circle

Everyone needs a Paul, everyone needs a Timothy.

He is a trusted accountant at Providence now, but Roy's life hasn't always been on track. He dropped out of high school a couple of decades ago, and drifted for the next eight years through a string of minimum-wage construction and factory jobs.

"I knew I had an alcohol problem by the time I was twenty-one," he laughed. "Just old enough to hit the bars, and already I was a mess." It's a distant memory now, but it wasn't so funny then. It was a continual, long, downward slide until finally, wanting a new direction in his life, he joined the Navy.

"That only lasted a year. I got an honorable discharge, but I was classified as a 'detox rehab failure.' After that I wandered aimlessly for several more years, cycling through countless rehab programs; Salvation Army, Denver Rescue Mission, Arapahoe CERT. On the street we call them "spin dry" programs, twenty eight days of intense detox that is intended to dry you out. Yeah, it didn't work for me."

"About 2001 I left the Denver Rescue Mission again, and found myself one night in one of those cheap, pay-by-the-week motels. I knew I had messed up. I called the Mission back to beg them to let me back in but I was on a 30-day bar from returning. I was desperate, at the end. I didn't know how to live drunk, didn't know how to live sober and was too much of a coward to commit suicide. Instead of taking my life, I got down on my knees in the motel room and asked Jesus to take over my life.

The next day I called another program to see if they would take me in again, but they turned me down because I had already failed their program several times. When I threatened suicide they took me in on a 72 hour lockdown. Long story short, God miraculously opened the doors after that for me to stay, I got clean and sober, took some accounting courses and ended up here at Providence by God's sovereign hand. He led me here, step by step."

Roy has volunteered now to be an ally in the Uprise program in order to give someone else the same kind of support and help he received to get his life together.

That someone was Steve.

Steve had been incarcerated for sixteen years, with seven of those years in solitary confinement. By his own admission he was a violent, angry person, but was graciously converted to Christ in prison through reading the Bible in a solitary confinement cell. After he was released in 2013, he ended up at Providence's Strong Tower Ministry, a program designed to help men and women get on their feet and stable after their release from prison. Eventually one of the staff invited both of them to join the Uprise program, a 12 month, high-intensity ministry that brings together "leaders" who want to lead their own way out of poverty with middle class "allies" who can mentor and support their journey. Roy became Steve's ally.

It has been a relational gift of God to each of them.

"We not only attend the training times together, but we hang out. We talk a lot about life, sobriety, what it means to walk with Jesus at this stage of life. We really have become friends. Steve even invited me to Thanksgiving with his extended family, which was a real treat for me. I help him work on his budget, since I am an accountant." He laughs. "He has helped me learn some things about myself too. I have my own poverty, like a lack of patience. Sometimes I get a little upset and impatient when I try to meet with him but he is doing something else, just because he is such a servant. He is always helping someone. I think maybe I need to learn a little bit about serving like him."

Steve graduated with top honors from the Uprise program. He now has a great job as a supervisor in construction, is stable, just bought a new truck and moved into his own apartment.

He now is wanting to be an ally in the Uprise program for someone else who wants to escape poverty.

Full circle.

"What I have declared to you, entrust to faithful men, who will be able to teach others also."
(2 Timothy 2:2)

What Are Your Addictions?

What makes you vulnerable makes you beautiful.

During a debrief with students who had been out on the streets for a poverty weekend, one young woman shared with the group how she had come face-to-face with dysfunctions she had never considered before.

Not those of the folks on the street, but her own.

She had struck up a conversation with a young twenty-something girl on the street who was strung out, talkative, and turning tricks to pay for her drug habits. Within five minutes she had told this college student all about her struggles with crack addiction, alcohol addiction, her abuse of prescription pills.

The student paused, then recounted the conversation. "After she had just told me all of this stuff about her addictions, she then asked me, with this incredible intensity, "And what are your addictions?" I was dumbfounded that she would assume that I had a drug problem. I stuttered and stumbled, and finally told her I didn't even smoke." Students laughed.

"Since then, though, I have been thinking about what things control me, but are just socially acceptable. Like needing people's approval. Or needing people to believe I am a good person, a moral person. That I am smart and educated. I'm definitely addicted to those things. And to material stuff. Oh my goodness! All of those things are like crack to me, drugs that control me and that I can't turn loose of. We're all broken, just in different ways."

No one laughed now. Others reflected on the destructiveness of their own socially acceptable, middle-class addictions.

"Those people" now on the street with their issues seemed less foreign, less strange. A spark of understanding flashed for a moment across people and social class.

On Reaching Muslims

...and when he saw him, he passed by on the other side.
(Luke 10:31)

My Malaysian friend is the student ministry director for a local university, and she was discussing with me the challenges associated with her ministry.

"I am often looking for churches in our community that would welcome our international students, not only Christians who need a "home-away-from-home" for worship and fellowship, but who would also welcome non-Christian students in order for them to get an exposure to Christianity. Before I do, of course, I attend first by myself to see how they react to me," she said.

"In many churches I am totally ignored, just invisible. I don't recommend those. I even attended a church seminar once on how to reach Muslims (Malaysia has a large Muslim population), and not only did no one speak to me, everyone avoided the pew where I sat. I discreetly texted a picture of my empty pew to some friends." She laughed. "And they want to reach Muslims!"

IV. NEW LENSES

Can You Help Me?

My times are in your hands.
(Psalm 31:15)

I was flying on the very day that Delta went bankrupt several years ago. They cancelled my flight, gave me $400 Delta dollars for a future flight and a $21 food voucher to use in the airport for food. The following flight they scheduled me for was cancelled, and they gave me *another* $400 Delta dollars and *another* $21 of food vouchers. A third flight was cancelled and *they gave me the same thing again.*

Question: What should I do with $63 worth of food vouchers in the airport? I certainly can't eat that much!

Answer: I thought about who could use this most. It wouldn't be other passengers; if they can afford to fly they don't need my food vouchers. I figured it would have to be workers in the airport, those who sweep up and clean the bathrooms maybe. Probably women more than men have the greatest need.

I approached a female worker in the terminal: "Excuse me, I had several flights cancelled this morning and they gave me a ton of food vouchers. Do you know anyone who could use these?"

I didn't say she looked like she worked at minimum wage cleaning bathrooms and looked like she could use them. To preserve her dignity, I asked her if she knew of anyone who could use them.

At first, she thought I was selling them.

"No, no," I said. "I'm just giving them away because I can't use them. Do you know of anyone, maybe?"

Her response: "Yes!" And so she took them. Actually, I didn't actually care if she knew someone or used them herself. That's not my responsibility. That's up to God.

The result ultimately was that someone benefited from the vouchers. I didn't waste them. No one was demeaned in the process. Perhaps she had been able to be an encouragement to someone else. It was a small success.

I was scheduled to teach in Beirut, Lebanon, a couple of months from then, and because of these cancelled flights and Delta dollars, God provided the flight for free.

God is sovereign and good.

Helping Without Insulting

"Your assumptions are your windows to the world. Scrub them off every once in a while, or the light won't come in."
Issac Asimov

I was walking downtown yesterday after a day at the library when a voice called out from behind me "Sir! Sir!" When I turned around, a sharply dressed woman following me thrust an aluminum-foil-wrapped-something up to my face and asked loudly, "Are you hungry, sir? Would you like a burrito?"

"No thank you," I responded and kept walking. I guess my $8 Goodwill oversized coat, backpack and stocking cap sends a certain signal.

I wasn't offended, and I don't fault her for being willing to do something for someone among the throngs of homeless people downtown. She meant well. But being on the receiving end of that exchange, it revealed a bit of how sometimes our offers of help can rob people of dignity. Imagine the self-respect I would have to give up at that moment to take her offer of a burrito. What did she do, with the best of intentions, that was awkward and dignity-robbing?

1. Calling out to me loudly on the street in a crowd and asking "Are you hungry?!" Translation: "Hey poor unknown man, you look to me like you could use my help. You look hungry." How much self-respect would I have to give up to admit instantly and publicly in a crowd "Why yes, well-dressed unknown woman, I do need help in providing

for my basic needs. I'm glad you can do that loudly and publicly, uninvited. What would you be so kind as to give me?"

2. Thrusting awkwardly an aluminum foil-wrapped burrito up to my face. First, sticking it in my face feels aggressive and disrespectful, regardless of how kindly you intended it. It's just your nerves probably, I know, talking to a person like me. But it does feel like a violation of my space. Maybe you should practice talking in front of a mirror until fear and nerves aren't so obvious. Really. Talk to me like a real person. I am one.

3. And besides, how do I know what it is you are sticking in my face? Is it your half-eaten leftover burrito from lunch? If you say "I would never do that!" how would I know? Many would and do. Do you think if I'm hungry I should be glad, even thankful for you to offer me half of your leftover burrito? That says something about how you view me as a person. I know already, I feel it. If I took it and discovered it actually was your half-eaten lunch you had given me like a dog being thrown leftovers, and I was less than enthusiastic with a thank you, would you be quick to tell me disgustedly, "Beggars can't be choosers!?"

I understand you want to help. And I might be hungry enough to lose a little more of my dignity and self-respect as a person to take it. But I won't feel good about it. And neither will you when I don't respond with appropriate good manners and a thank you. I will just be one more example of an ungrateful person that didn't appreciate your willingness to help.

Helping without hurting or insulting is hard.

Who Exactly Are the Poor?

No part of the Body has the right to say, I have no need of you.
(I Corinthians 12)

In Upstream Impact, one of our poverty alleviation programs at Providence, we bring the poor and middle class together in mutually beneficial, mentoring relationships. In weekly, structured relationships and activities spanning 12-18 months, everybody discovers something astonishing about themselves. They each discover they are poor, only in different ways, and each discovers how they have been damaged, either by oppression or privilege.

Damaged by privilege? Is that even possible?

Go around a room full of middle-class people and ask them to name, other than family, three people whom they know are in their corner if they hit a crisis. Who are the three people they could call at 3:00 a.m. if their mother died, or they were diagnosed with cancer, or their child was jailed or killed in a car accident?

Because privilege emphasizes self-sufficiency, the middle-class often tend to be so isolated they have no deep friendships, only acquaintances. The poor, on the other hand, may lack finances, but they often are marked by rich relational networks. You need others to survive.

Until that realization, middle-class folks tend to have a savior mentality who come to "help those poor folks." It is a revelation to discover that we are all broken, only in different ways, and that we are all rich, only in different ways. It's only then that the ground is recognized as level and folks can begin to learn from and mentor each other.

The poor not only need us. We need the poor.

Context

Then the Lord asked me, "What do you see?"
(Jeremiah 24:3)

Moses pastored a largely unemployed, blue-collar community of migrants (former mud-brick laborers) in a bad neighborhood for forty years on food stamps called manna.

Does this sound odd to your ear? It shouldn't.

If my reading of the Bible is essentially always through the lens of American, middle-class, dominant culture and its particular issues, I will struggle to minister meaningfully outside of that bubble.

In other words, if I unconsciously see Moses as a white, middle-class pastor with a white middle-class congregation facing white, middle-class problems, I not only will miss much of the emphasis/richness of the biblical text, I will be clueless in cross-cultural situations as to why people are tepid in their response to my ministry, see me and Scripture as irrelevant, or actually resist me as an outsider who is likely coming to exploit.

They may not be resistant to the Spirit, I may just be culturally incompetent or irrelevant.

Doing Church Right

It is not good to have zeal without knowledge.
(Proverbs 19:2)

On Sunday my artsy, multi-talented friend Allyson recounted to me her university assignment of drawing a model seated in the center of the classroom. Her observation: Every student in the class drew the same person, yet every drawing was unique.

Which view was the "right" one?

Opening Day of baseball season was yesterday for many teams. In any given stadium across the nation, everyone watched the same game, yet all saw it from different positions in the stands. Those behind home plate got a different view and experience of the game than the shortstop, or those in the outfield stands.

Which view of the game was the "right" one?

Last night I was on a panel with two African-American scholars and pastors discussing race and racism with a white, suburban, Presbyterian church.

Which view on these issues was the "right" one?

The church had organized this panel discussion because they are genuinely interested in understanding the faith from other cultural perspectives. Their invitation was a first step towards discovery; "How can you all help us understand racism, race, faith and the family of God? We want to learn, help us to see what we don't see."

It was an engaging evening. It is particularly crucial for theologically conservative, dominant-culture churches such as this one to be proactive in gaining diverse perspectives. According to Michael Emerson, author of *Divided By Faith*, the more theologically conservative a church is, the more mono-cultural and racially isolated they tend to be.

That has had significant consequences, one of which is that isolation tends to passively reinforce the view that a church's own cultural expression is "the" right way to do church. Preferences become subtly promoted to biblical principles, and consequently, any deviation from the standard way of doing things is thought to be a departure from the faith, an incremental and inevitable slide toward liberalism. Much like the Judaizers in Acts 15, they tend to believe not only that others must believe like they believe, but they must also practice the faith as they do to be faithful. Such narrow perspectives lead to further isolation as they are wary of and separate from those they believe to be unbiblical.

Learning to value the rich panorama and texture of cultural expressions does not change the essential nature of the gospel any more than observing the game in the stadium from different positions change the essential nature of baseball. It does, however, deeply enrich one's appreciation of it.

Poverty of Trusting People

"Wanting to alleviate pain without sharing it is like wanting to save a child from a burning building without the risk of being hurt."
H. Nouwen

"If poverty means to lack something, what kinds of poverty are there besides lack of finances?" I ask. People call out:

"Poverty of deep friendships."
"Poverty of emotional resources."
"Poverty of community."
"Poverty of self-image, or self-worth."

Comments continue, and then eventually, ideas exhausted, the room falls silent. Hesitantly, a final soft voice ventures a perspective born of experience:

"Poverty of trusting people."

It was a powerful moment.

That's why working with the poor is not drive-by ministry. You don't earn trust overnight.

Thundering Herd

If all were a single member, where would the body be?
There are many parts, yet one body.
(I Corinthians 12:20)

In my high school band there were probably 100 kids. Apparently because of some grievous sin in a previous life of our new band director, there were - count them - 25 drummers. I was one of them.

It could not have been a worse assignment for a new teacher. It certainly could not have been the dream job he envisioned, fresh from college, as he stood at the threshold of his new career.

His daily task throughout that school year was attempting to reign in a thundering percussion section. Just through sheer numbers we dominated everything. Regardless of what we played, no matter how he tried to instill in us the distinctions between pianissimo and fortissimo, everything sounded like Alabama's Crimson Tide drum line at halftime. Of course we loved to play, and loved to hear ourselves play. It was all us, all the time, loud and proud.

It was fun, if you were a drummer. If you were in the brass or woodwind section, however, it was a nightmare. Discouraged and exasperated, other kids played well and all had important parts to contribute to the music, but were overpowered by 25 energetic freshmen simply doing what they loved to do.

It wasn't mean spirited. We weren't bullies. We weren't intentionally trying to dominate and alienate everyone else in that rehearsal room. The result, however, was the same. It was just us being us, a dominant group of kids in a percussion section doing what we knew.

We had no clue about valuing or listening to others around us in the band. We hadn't learned to adjust our own volume to those whose contributions were softer and harder to hear in the presence of such overpowering numbers. The importance of blending our unique contributions with others to produce something greater and more beautiful than any of us individually was lost in our dominating, thunderous presence.

We drummers played and encouraged each other with how good we sounded. We didn't have a clue why others were frustrated and unhappy. Didn't they appreciate band? Maybe they should just join the chess club or something if they didn't like to play.

I am ashamed now that we never wrestled at the time with how our dominance affected others in the band. What did those kids think who wanted to play and contribute as much as we did, but had to tolerate daily our loud, overbearing presence? What did those two timid young girls who played oboe think about us, for example, or those mellow-sounding French horns? How angry was that row of clarinet players who constantly glared at us, so tense and upright on the edge of their straight-back chairs? Were they exasperated every single day with us? How discouraging was it not only to have to work hard to learn your instrument and music like everyone else, but also to simply try to be heard and valued as part of the band?

If you have ever been in a multi-cultural ministry context, you know this is not just a story about drummers and a high school band. It is a lesson for all dominant-culture folks in a multi-cultural church. How overbearing is our presence? How much do we crush, unintentionally or otherwise, and sometimes with the best of intentions, the voices and instruments of others in the orchestra? How oblivious might we be to those around us?

Thundering Herd II

This issue of power is one of the most important aspects to address when working in a multi-ethnic context. Any church that is multi-ethnic with a dominant group faces the same challenges. How does a dominant group keep from dominating?

It is a constant challenge for everyone to bring what they have to offer to the table, but yet to do so in a way that neither minimizes one's own perspective nor overpowers the voice and presence of others. Everyone has something to offer, and the sum is greater than the parts. That is a goal worth intentionally pursuing, but hard to balance.

We can fall in a ditch on either side of the road. One extreme is for minority voices to capitulate to dominant groups and refuse to bring their unique contribution to the mix. Either through passivity or assimilation, the value of diversity evaporates. On the other hand, majority groups must be alert to how much their domination and control, intentional or unintentional, feels like a heavy blanket that covers and stifles everything.

Unless this default dynamic of dominant group control is acknowledged and skillfully addressed, ministries will always tend to default to the control and influence of the dominant group. This stance need not be hostile. Indeed, it may be quite benevolent, subtle, and couched in spiritual terms. The bottom line, however, is that if the use of power is not addressed, some groups will be marginalized while others will dominate by default. Everyone will suffer, and God's agenda will be hindered.

Questions we must ask ourselves to move forward together in a diverse context:

1. Do all ethnic groups and both genders sense their views are heard in the larger group? Do they feel it is a 'safe' place to speak honestly? Is space made to intentionally invite other voices into the conversation? Do they feel their contributions are valued? Seriously considered? Or do people sense that if they are 'not a drummer,' they will be marginalized anyway and it won't matter? Are concerns raised by minority members dismissed out-of-hand, or worse, subtly challenged as being 'divisive'?

2. How are decisions made? Is there a willingness to make strategic decisions based on standards other than majority vote? Are dominant culture folks willing to stretch in pursuit of an agenda that not only embraces but proactively pursues diversity? Are they willing to sacrifice to make room for leaders from outside of the dominant group in order to fulfill God's bigger agenda?

3. Are people willing to embrace and champion this emphasis on diversity, or do they simply passively consent to it, or even subtly resist it?

4. Are there structures in place whereby concerns can be voiced without being ostracized?

A crucial role in that symphonic band was the leadership role of the band director. As the leader, he held a significant place of influence. Timidly at first, then with growing confidence, he stepped into his role as a change agent. Explaining, challenging, coaching, correcting, and sometimes even confronting our drum section daily, he guided us over time into becoming a team of drummers that contributed to the success and purpose of the whole band.

Easy? Hardly. But the results over time were profound.

On the other hand, he also had to learn how to coach the rest of the band, a demoralized group that had become settled in their frustration, apathetic and defensive. Those who had been consistently dominated, marginalized and overpowered were, as is often the case, slow to respond. Those on that end of the continuum had to be coached through some hard, character-forming lessons as well, such as learning to give people room to grow as well as room to fail.

They had to work on patience with the process of change, forgiving people when the growth trajectory of others didn't reflect a consistently upward arrow but a rather jagged, struggling one.

Henry Ford is often quoted as saying "Coming together is a beginning. Staying together is progress. Working together is success."

That doesn't happen by accident. It takes work. Forgiveness. Patience. Commitment to a common purpose. A lot of leadership. A lot of humility and submission to the Spirit.

In the end, though, the results are priceless. There is no substitute for the sweeping, magnificent orchestral impact of such unity in diversity.

'No part of the body has the right to say, I have no need of you." (I Cor 12:13)

Slow Growth

"You can't move things by not moving."
Suzy Kssem

Helping people escape generational poverty is a lot like helping people to know Jesus. It takes patience. A lot of patience.

The problem is, we *like* the idea of instant change. We *want* instant change. We *expect* instant change.

How often do people in certain circles talk of *radical transformation* at the point of conversion: "I came to Jesus and put down the (choose one: *bottle *crackpipe *needle *porn *anger *all of the above) and it's never been a problem for me again! Praise Jesus!"

C'mon. That *might* be the case, sometimes. On the other hand, some of us have been around the block. I've been in ministry 40 years. God *could* do that, but that's not usually the way it is.

That "magic moment" model of changed lifestyle at conversion that people love to hear; i.e. "Wow, the old is passed away, everything is new!" in my opinion is a bit like Santa Claus. No one has seen him, everyone knows he is not real, but everyone kind of plays along as if he is.

More often than not, one commits to Jesus first, the Spirit moves in, and their values and actions change over time. The desire to do certain things is gradually replaced by the desire to do differently. Like renovating a house, you take a brick out, put a brick in; take a board out, put a board in. It's called "progressive sanctification." Because they want Jesus and want a different lifestyle, eventually there IS clearly a different lifestyle. Not perfect, but different. People notice.

(OK, don't write me to protest. Maybe *you* were instantly sanctified. Most weren't.)

Development among the poor is the same way.

The poor don't instantly overcome their issues now that they know Jesus. It takes time, often a long time. They need good teachers (like you did), strong models (like you did), strong support (like you did), and time (like you did), in order to turn the corner and set a different life trajectory.

When we are aware of this we, or donors, won't burden the poor or those who minister among them with unrealistic, middle-class, North American, microwave expectations of instant spiritual/social success.

Change comes, just not at warp-speed. The kingdom is slow-growing, so stop expecting otherwise.

It's going to take longer, be harder, and cost you more than we expected.

Worth It

"You may encounter many defeats, but you must not be defeated. In fact, it may be necessary to encounter the defeats, so you can know who you are, what you can rise from, how you can still come out of it."
Maya Angelou

To hear people gush about their change of direction in life after years of defeat, discouragement, and bad choices does something wonderful to your spirit.

Hang around here and you will meet them; men and women excited about life, people who are taking control of their own lives and future and leaving generational poverty behind. Some plod on their journey, others roar at full-throttle.

Christy (not her real name), a woman in one of our programs, knows full throttle. She was ecstatic as she told us about the welding class she was just finishing. Excitedly she ticked off on her fingers the various kinds of welding; oxygen, TIG, MIG, Stick, Flux-cored Arc, Acetylene. She hardly stopped to catch her breath.

We looked at each other finally, then at her, and burst out laughing. "We know you are speaking English, but we have no idea what you are saying."

She laughed. What she really wanted, she said, was to take the next course of pipe welding that would enable her to make significantly more money. Hands-on training would be an additional six months or so, which would be a big commitment for someone not used to a classroom.

"Wow, it might be boring for you to be in a classroom for another six months," my friend cautioned.

She howled in laughter. "I JUST SPENT THREE AND A HALF YEARS IN PRISON! I CAN HANDLE A LITTLE BOREDOM! THIS BOREDOM IS GETTING ME A GOOD PAYING JOB!"

Self-sufficiency. Self-confidence. Success in accomplishing a big goal, joy in life, finally. Laughter among friends solidly in her corner.

She used to be seen by society just as one more ex-offender, a felon with no skills and no job. Having a front-row seat to witness her transformation is priceless.

You Can't Rush Understanding

"'The map is not the territory,' Snicket's chaperone advises him. 'That's an expression which means the world does not match the picture in our heads.'"
Lemony Snicket

"Explain to us the miracle of the boats!"

My friend in the mountains of Guatemala had recently begun discipling these men who were now gathered outside of his hut. They had been reading the Bible together and now had questions.

He was puzzled. "Wait. What? What miracle of the boats?"

"You know, the one in John 6." One man quoted it. "'*Then some boats from Tiberias landed near the place where the people had eaten the bread.*' Please, help us to understand the purpose of that miracle.'"

Puzzled, he thought for a minute. "Oh!" he said as the light clicked on. "I see what you mean. Come on inside and let's talk."

What did he see in that text that now made him understand his friend's question?

The text says, "Some boats from Tiberias landed near the place where the people had eaten…" He recognized that what it *doesn't* say is that people were in the boats. If you believe that people sailed those boats across the lake, it is an implication of your worldview and English grammar. That is not what the text says. You *assume* people sailed the boats because your worldview tells you that boats don't sail themselves.

On the other hand, it makes total sense to believe, if you have been steeped in an animist culture like these men, that unmanned boats made a trip by themselves across the lake. Why? Because animists believe that spirits inhabit inanimate objects all the time and make such objects move at will. From *their* animist backgrounds, it was *totally reasonable* to assume that the boats just made their *own* way across the lake. They didn't question the event, they just questioned the purpose.

Can you see the difficulty of clashing worldviews?

Wherever you are in cross cultural ministry, people's beliefs and actions, whether wise or not, make total sense to *them* even though they may not make sense to US.

For example, among the poor:

Why a big screen TV but on government assistance?
Why 20" chrome rims on your car but your electric got turned off?
Why fast food when you could buy three times that amount of food in the grocery?
Why does your kid sleep on the floor, but you have an IPhone?

There are places that God will want to take us as we learn from their worldview. But it will not do to simply condemn what we don't understand. We must understand their worldview and enter their world to grasp why people think and act as they do. We must start with where people are if we are ever to get where God wants to take us - together.

Winter

You turned my mourning into dancing.
(Psalm 30:11)

There was a bitter wind as I walked around the lake tonight. I pulled my hoodie tighter.

Not too long ago I was in a T-shirt and shorts on my familiar, nightly walk. Now it's a sweatshirt, field jacket and stocking cap. It's gotten colder.

I reflected back on the summer as I leaned into the brisk headwind in the dark. So different! So many people surrounded me in the park then; kickball leagues, joggers, walkers, picnickers, hand-holders, Frisbee-tossers, dog-walkers in the fading light. I passed wedding receptions in the pavilion with oldies, the Electric Slide, laughter, toasts.

Now it's just dark. Quiet. Even the fountains are still. I'm alone. I don't see or meet anyone else. It seems I am the only one in the whole park.

My thoughts turn to dear friends who have experienced this kind of transition in their lives, from life and energy to darkness and solitude, from and celebration to loneliness and silence. These are friends whose marriages have gone south, ministries that are done because of bad choices, friendships wrecked, dreams dashed, all seemingly for good. It's dark and cold.

Winter is real, but it is not eternal. Spring will come.

Darkness to light, death to life, grief to joy, sadness to laughter.

It will come.

Your darkness, says Jesus, is not terminal. It will lift.

It's why he came.

Living with No Answers

"Waiting on God requires the willingness to bear uncertainty, to carry within oneself the unanswered question, lifting the heart to God about it whenever it intrudes upon one's thoughts."
Elisabeth Elliot

Sitting at the Charlotte airport, waiting. Hope and despair flicker alternately on a neon flight board. My thoughts drift to how much of life is spent like this.

Everyone learns to wait.

As a kid you wait interminably; for Christmas morning, for school to be out for the summer, the dentist.

As a teen you wait, counting the hours, until you are old enough to drive. You wait to graduate high school, wait to leave for college, wait to finally be on your own.

In your twenties you wait still; to afford your first apartment, for commencement, for a job interview, for someone. Often that is a dreary wait and gray; for many not only is there no "ring by spring," there is no one on the horizon. Months turn to years for some who come home alone every night to a quiet apartment full of unanswered questions. Others transition to a whole different kind of waiting; for "Ode to Joy" to begin, for a positive test, for water to break, for first words, first steps, first day of kindergarten. Still others wait for papers to be served and court dates; for ashes to morph into different dreams.

Waiting gets more complex as you get older; waiting for a promotion or pink slip, for a teen out late to get home, lab reports from elderly parents, telephone calls with somber news; nights in dim hospital rooms, huddles with specialists; long hours tag-teaming beside hospice beds. Waiting for the service to begin. It is a discipline learned reluctantly.

God's waiting room is where life is lived though, and where character and faith are forged. Sometimes we forget that we don't wait alone.

Pulling Back the Curtain

The two most important days in life; the day you were born the day you figure out why.

In the fluorescent light of memory now, it is difficult to express the depth of it. It was such an intimate, personal experience with God that I have hesitated to share it with people, mostly out of fear that the sacredness of the moment would be cheapened by sarcastic comments or lame humor. Some moments you protect.

I have forgotten the airport, but I was walking to my connecting flight through a rather long, narrow walkway that connected terminals. I was exhausted. One more flight and I would finally be home to my family, to warmth and love and hugs.

The narrow walkway had obviously been rather recently renovated, with two parallel moving-sidewalks down the center of the concourse, one in each direction. Overhead, the length of the terminal was a rainbow of artsy colored lights, long thin tubes twisted in abstract shapes radiating brilliant tones. The sound that wrapped around us wasn't music, but rather, dissonant tones that together with the lighting produced a kind of surreal, all-enveloping visual and acoustical experience.

I stepped onto the moving sidewalk, dropped my computer case heavily at my feet and leaned on the black handrail. I had time. I would rest my weary feet for the hundred yard trip.

Several flights must have recently arrived, because the opposite sidewalk was loaded with people, talking, laughing, or texting. They were families, businessmen and women, grandparents, single travelers, mothers herding children, bored teens with headphones, an excited high school sports team.

Suddenly, inexplicably, for an instant everything seemed in suspended animation. In hindsight it was probably just a few seconds, but during those moments I had an incredibly heightened sense of reality, an acute awareness that I was seeing something deeply significant.

God seemed to say, "Pay attention. I'm showing you something."

The freeze-framed picture was brilliantly clear. Just a few of us were on the walkway I was on, headed home. But so, so many were headed in the opposite direction. I heard no words, but the meaning I felt in the core of my being.

As I watched them all pass me by, preoccupied and oblivious, I nearly burst out in tears.

Wide is the gate and broad is the road that leads to destruction. But small is the gate and narrow the road that leads to life, and only a few find it.
(Matthew 7:13)

Pain in the Offering

"Love will cost you dearly. And it will break your heart. But in the end, it will save the world."
Sarah Thebarge

Who would have believed this was part of God's call on a young girl's life?

It was just so relentless. So unjustified, this continual heavy blanket of social isolation. Such cold disdain. Such painful, emotional distancing from the only community she had ever known.

Mary was young, pregnant, and now an outsider. That's what happens when you sleep around.

She would soon discover that those difficult days would not just be during the early months as she began to show. Her life of obedience would bring her a life of exclusion. It was a lonely journey that stretched far past delivery. Even after that sweet boy was born she, like all new mothers, must have longed to hear those weighty words of affirmation and approval from the only endorsing agency that mattered; mothers and grandmothers. Ah, to see them chatter and fawn over her boy, stroking his face and hands, clucking to each other how beautiful he was and what a fine son he would be!

That would not happen. She felt the resistance from the beginning. That's what happens when you sleep around.

Did she tire of the subtle, contemptible rolling of the eyes when she came around? Did 'good folks' feign weak, obligatory smiles in her direction at Temple? Did respectable folks whisper and nod in her direction as she wandered through the market? Did parents huff and sniff as they guided their young ones away from such a girl in the village?

Well. That's what happens when you sleep around.

Especially telling about Mary's lifelong pain as a result of her obedience is reflected later in a sharp exchange between her son and the Pharisees 30 years later.

Jesus had confronted the Pharisees about their resistance to spiritual truth as leaders, their confidence being in their heritage instead of God. So proud to be Abraham's children.

Jesus' challenge cut to the quick: "If you were Abraham's children you would do the works of Abraham."

They erupted into a furious rage and insulted him in the worst possible terms they could imagine: They insulted his mother.

"*We* were not born of fornication!" they sneer. It is an assault on Mary.

"Who are you to teach us anything?! *We* are educated, respectable, leaders in the community. And who are you, Jesus? You are nothing. Worse than nothing. You, Jesus, are an uneducated, homeless bastard. We remember you. We were around when you were born, you son of a whore! And *you* want to teach *us*?!" They mock.

Thirty years later the story surrounding the birth of her son is still a painful part of her life in community.

Is that just what happens when you sleep around? Or is the majestic, life-altering call of God on a person's life often a call to suffer for a larger agenda?

Ask Mary.

Waiting

"What we are waiting for is not as important as what happens to us while we are waiting."
Mandy Hale

"When two full years had passed..." *Genesis 41:1*

For two years after Joseph fully expected God to miraculously and imminently intervene and deliver him from his prison cell, God did nothing of the kind. Wrongfully accused. Wrongfully convicted. Wrongfully imprisoned. And yet the Sovereign Over All sat on his hands. And Joseph sat in prison.

What did Joseph think every day during those two years? What thoughts preoccupied his mind through every long, cold, bone-chilling, never-ending, lonely night on that stone floor? Week after mind-numbing week, month after pointless month through painfully dull and colorless months and seasons, what did he think about God? Was he convinced God had forgotten him? Did he get bitter? Fight depression? Did his faith grow dim? Did he doubt?

Whatever he faced, it reflects those endless times many of us have faced as we waited on God to deliver us:

from singleness.
from unemployment.
from marital issues. Child issues.
from health issues.
from sinful and dark times framed by life choices.

If history is any indication, God is working behind the scenes with a plan bigger than what you know.

Don't take my word for it. That's Genesis 41.

V. BEAUTY AND BROKENNESS

You Gotta Know This Place to Fix It

Live here. Love here. Lament here. Listen here.

Those who speak loudest and with the most confidence about 'simple solutions' for complex problems are typically those who have the least contact and personal investment in the situation.

In fact, there is often an inverse relationship between how little exposure people have to poor, urban communities, and yet how confident they are of solutions for its challenges.

Live here. Love here. Lament here. Listen here.

Then you will not speak 'to' an abstract, faceless community. You will speak about solutions 'with' friends you love in community.

What Do You See?

"God tells you where to look; love tells you what to see."
Matshona Dhilwayo

What would you have seen if you had run with me through the Memphis neighborhood that I did at dawn this morning?

I'll tell you what I saw. Abandoned buildings. Trash in the street. Broken glass on the sidewalk. Quick Cash offices. Empty lots, high weeds. Neglected playgrounds. Project housing.

But as often happens during a run, God poked me to see more than the obvious.

"What else do you see, Jeff? Can you only see blight here? Where are the signs of life and community and joy here?"

Like one of those trick pictures where you might see either an old woman or a horse's head depending on how hard you look, I began to really concentrate on what I was seeing as I ran.

The signs were already everywhere, I just hadn't seen them; the childcare facility with the colorful, hand lettered sign in the yard, the barbershops, the multiple youth centers on every block. Signs of entrepreneurial neighbors were everywhere also, as seen by the small car repair garages, hair and nail shops, one room storefronts with names like King Grocery, named after the martyr murdered just blocks from this neighborhood. Scattered along every block also were centers of hope and healing for families called health clinics, dental offices and churches, all seeming to have sprung up like grass through cracks in the pavement.

You see what you expect to see.

On Fixing People

"It's a dangerous business, Frodo, going out your door. You step out onto the road, and if you don't keep your feet, there's no knowing where you might be swept off to."
J.R.R. Tolkien

The house we just bought has a huge spot of dead grass in the yard. It's rather obvious, and rather ugly. Everything else is lush green, and this is dead and brown. I should do something.

Amateur that I am, I guess the problem. Grubs? Moles? Fertilizer? Dig it up and re-seed? Maybe I just need to go ahead and get a professional to deal with it and not waste time and money guessing. Oh man, I wonder. How expensive are those guys?

My friend Jerome the landscaper stops by. He sees the spot, scans the surrounding yard and offhandedly says "That huge pine tree is sucking all the water from that area. It's dying of thirst. Just water it. It'll be O.K."

That's it? That's all? Anxious to "fix" things, I could have been taking all kinds of serious and expensive action that would not have addressed my problem at all.

It makes me wonder how often I have been wrong in years of ministry and counseling, doing all of the things that I thought should be done with someone that didn't really get to the source of some problem? The older I get, the more I realize that before I start 'fixing' things, especially people, I had better understand the real issues. They are not always the presenting problem. I am reminded that it can be dangerous to hurry in ministry, because I often don't know what I don't know. That takes time, wisdom and insight to discover.

I certainly understand that in other areas of life. I have been suitably and rightfully irritated when I have taken my car in for repairs somewhere and some mechanic has started fixing something on my car that turned out not to be the problem at all. At the end of the day I not only had less money, I had the same problem.

On the other hand, even though it makes me impatient and anxious if I go to the doctor and they send me for endless tests before they actually diagnose a problem, I understand it. I want them to hurry up and just tell me what my issue is, but they are insistent and wisely err on the side of caution. They take time. They want to understand. They want to be sure what my problem *isn't* in the process of determining what my problem is. Ultimately I am glad they do.

If we are careful to be that cautious in the physical realm, how much more important is it in the spiritual?

Why We Stayed

Resisting the Holy Huddle

He and I sat together one evening balancing paper plates of lasagna on our knees in community group. I was visiting for the first time, and we had just been introduced. We made small talk as we ate. He and his family had been at the church three years already; we had just recently begun attending. I was curious. "What convinced you to stay at Providence?" I queried.

"When a homeless guy fell asleep across the chairs next to me the first time we visited, I knew this was the place for us," he said. "We've been here ever since."

We laughed. We laughed because it was such a striking and clear value statement about what a church should be as a place of acceptance and welcome. Economic class, gender, ethnicity, addictions, marital status, a myriad of other characteristics and distinctions that separate people into categories and classes should have no sway in the community of Jesus followers.

An accepting and welcoming environment, of course, is not inconsistent with calling people to grow and change. The community of believers is to be a place where people collectively commit to grow together; spiritually, emotionally, and intellectually. The paradox, however, is this:

"People can only change when they feel accepted for the way they are now." – John Kuypers

This is a discussion every church should have regularly. Do we communicate a communal, family atmosphere where people genuinely feel accepted as they are, or do they feel they must first stop being who they are in order to be loved or belong? Do they sense that they must somehow first clear pre-determined, unspoken hurdles in order to be accepted? Should the homeless guy, for example, have gotten his act together first before he ventured a visit to the church?

That is a hard conversation, but a necessary one if people are to eventually feel safe enough to risk change. In a multi-ethnic context especially, we will have to talk about nurturing an environment where people feel culturally respected, accepted and affirmed. Latino? Asian? African–American? White? Native-American? The message we must be careful to continuously send is this, "Welcome! We accept you, love you, and are thankful for you. We value what you bring to the table. You help us to become more of what God wants the Church family to be. Come, let us live together and enrich each other as we seek to serve and reflect the creative diversity of God together in a broken world. Travel this road together with us. We need you."

Unless that is true, the walls remain high and buttresses strong.

Investing

"Sometimes it takes God a long time to work 'suddenly.'"
Bill Johnson

It was dawn and a brisk early morning walk when I circled the perimeter of a city golf course in Denver. Huge, 100 year old oaks and maples lined the fairways and street. Beautiful, stable, thick with foliage, they provide shade and striking beauty not only for golfers but for so many here in this community.

I continued to walk, and on the far side of the course I came upon trees that were mostly slender saplings, recently planted. Spindly, no doubt vulnerable and needing a lot of care and nurture in the summer sun that blazes so hot at this elevation. Someone had also carefully wired them for stability during the harsh Denver winters.

Tap. Tap. God might as well have spoken verbally.

"Another generation planted all of those tall, mature oaks and maples. All of the work, care and nurture of those trees a hundred years ago was done by people who themselves would never enjoy their shade or beauty. Theirs was an investment of faith, looking toward the future.

Those saplings? They are also careful investments in the future by workers in the present who will not live to see the benefits. By faith, however, their labor and sweat will enable those slender young trees to become oaks, benefiting a coming generation with shade and the beauty of their presence."

It was a sacred and precious moment in which I felt God was saying something to me about our recent move to Denver and a new ministry.

"You are immersing and pouring yourselves into a broken community with people who are often vulnerable, on the margins and in need of stabilizing support and growth. Growth seems sometimes as slow as the growth of an oak tree. What potential there is, however, for a redeemed community to provide beauty and blessing for others now and in years to come! You may not see the ultimate outcome in your lifetime, but what you do here is important. Just remember not to judge yourself or others simply by how things look at the moment."

That is good to remember when you are growing oak trees.

Bonsai Ministry

"If you don't know what your barriers are, it's impossible to figure out how to tear them down."
John Manning

A model for us at Providence as we minister among the poor is the bonsai tree.

There is actually no such thing as a bonsai tree, it is a methodology. Pick a seed from the tallest-growing tree in the forest and plant it in a small bonsai pot. It's growth will be so restricted that instead of a towering tree it will only grow a few inches. It is not a problem with the seed's potential, it's a problem with its environment.

Here in Denver through our programs among the poor, we are helping to break the pots that restrict our neighbor's economic, relational and spiritual growth. If you live and work among the poor you know that most of the restrictive "pots" in people's lives are not easily or quickly shattered. A few of the restrictions that we encounter are the equivalent of clay pots, easily broken to free the root systems. Far more often, however, the pots are like cast iron or carved granite. It takes perseverance, endurance, and relentless strength to break them. Sometimes it takes a tag team of several people working together to pound away continuously with the right, heavy duty tools. Good intentions aren't enough. A timid karate chop or a rubber mallet won't do. It often takes strong, repeated, strategic blows over time with a ten pound sledgehammer at full force to break free. Of course, it also takes a plant that is willing to endure, participates in the process and wants to be free, no matter the cost.

Development is hard work. The flourishing and beautiful tree that now grows strong and tall, however, is worth it.

Power and Injustice

"I guess the only time most people think about injustice is when it happens to them."
Charles Bukowski

My friend Michelle Warren states it well; "If you wake up every morning to a system that works for you, you believe that it's a pretty good system."

What about those who do not wake up to the same world? Many middle-class, dominant culture Christians have few relationships with those who wake up every day to a parallel universe, and therefore simply don't believe them when they hear them describe a much different reality. Their attitude communicates disbelief, "If it has not been my experience, then it cannot be true."

A common area of disbelief by those who have never experienced it is the abuse of power by law enforcement. The disbelief and resistance of many is often rooted in their own personal relationship with someone in law enforcement or the judicial system who is honest, ethical, and deeply committed to justice.

That of course does not prove the impossibility of injustice with the system itself. In fact, the Bible argues strongly that the powerless experience injustice at the hands of those in power in practically every book of the Bible. For example:

Joseph. Unjustly imprisoned.
Jeremiah. Unjustly imprisoned.
Daniel. Unjustly imprisoned.

John. Unjustly imprisoned.
Paul. Unjustly imprisoned.
John the Baptist. Unjustly imprisoned, executed.
James. Unjustly imprisoned, executed.
The apostles. Unjustly imprisoned, executed.
Jesus. Unjustly imprisoned, executed.

Every single one of these biblical characters were on the receiving end of abuse by those in power.

If Christians read the Bible with integrity, they must affirm that the potential of systemic abuse at the hands of power is always present. The history of Egypt, Babylon, and Rome all testify to abuse of the powerless at the hands of the powerful.

Today, however, many who claim the name of Jesus deny such abuse takes place, and even blindly *defend* the institutions of power that abuse.

You Can't Un-see

"If your goal is to produce firefighters and rescue workers, you have to produce people willing to enter burning buildings."
Brian McLaren

I am wondering, as some have suggested, if lack of exposure leads to passivity.

Is it possible that Moses never wrestled with the plight of the Israelites before he was 40 years old because he never saw them, never had to think about them? His passivity would have continued had he not chosen to personally enter the world of the Hebrew slaves.

Afterwards, however, I wonder if Moses ever lay awake at night, wishing he could go back to the "good old days" in the palace when life was easier; when he didn't have to wrestle deep in his soul with these dark and awful issues of oppression, exploitation and violence.

There was a time when he didn't have to think about such things; they were invisible to him. Raised in the royal court of Egypt, he knew nothing of the daily, oppressive existence of two million people who suffered daily under the heavy hand of Pharaoh. He was insulated, protected. Of course he knew OF them. But he didn't have to deal *with* them. They weren't his concern. His entire life had been one of privilege. Wealth was his only frame of reference, power his only experience, a life carefully isolated from having to face the daily reality of "those people."

But then he saw what he saw. Flagrant oppression, sickening violence. Power used by the powerful against the powerless. He couldn't help it. It tripped a switch. There was no denying, no rationalizing. The witnessing of such violence at the hand of power was a turning point for this man raised in affluence and privilege. He could have walked away in denial. He could have blocked his ears, averted his eyes, rationalized, justified, gone back to the palace and to his own version of normal.

But he couldn't un-see what he had seen. It changed his life.

And everything else.

Help and Hope After Prison

I'm here. I'll walk with you.

James* can tell you what it is like to be an ex-offender. Having served time for a felony conviction, he has had not only 'Department of Corrections' on the back of his shirt for years, it has seemingly been imprinted on his heart and DNA.

He can describe for you in excruciating detail what it feels like to be without hope. Even though he paid his debt to society with his prison term, and even though he knows Jesus and wants to do right at this point and lead a different life, he knows he is a branded man.

Felon.

Of course he has heard *ad nauseam* all of the classic criticisms from those who have never been in his shoes. He knows the dismissive tone, the astonishing arrogance and naïveté of those who have never been where he is: "I see help wanted signs everywhere! People can work if they want to. They just don't want to. Those people are just lazy and want to live off of my tax dollars."

Fresh from prison, he will tell you about every job application he has ever filled out, and the final question on every form: "Have you ever been convicted of a felony? If so, please explain." He knows he will not get a call after that. Oh, they will smile and tell him they will review his application. They will promise to get back to him. They will wish him a nice day. The call will never come. He knows that.

Two weeks ago, on the day he faced eviction from his apartment, James wandered into Strong Tower, our ministry for citizens returning from incarceration. He was out of money, out of options, out of friends, and facing life back on the street. Through tears at his first visit to our Thursday evening worship service, he shared that he was on the verge of going back to dealing drugs. He hated it. He knew where it could lead. He had been there before. But when you have no money, no resources, no safety net and few options for work even at a minimum wage job, you do desperate things to survive.

Yes, he needed help, but he also needed hope, the sense that someone cared about what happened to him.

Strong Tower had recently gotten a grant from the VA for assisting veterans who struggle with homelessness and the challenges of being an ex-offender. It gave them what they needed to keep him in his apartment, connect him to some resources, nurture his relationship with the church and point him to Jesus again.

It was God's people who were there waiting when he hit bottom.

If one of you says to them, "Go in peace; keep warm and well fed,"
but does nothing about their physical needs, what good is it?
(James 2:16)

Invisible Injustice

"Is it nothing to you, all ye who pass by?"
(Lamentations 1:12)

Within 24 hours of the violent execution of this innocent man by the state, those in power scrambled to cover up this entire spectacle of injustice by a scheming bribe of the law enforcement officials. They paid them to lie, coached them along in their lie for consistency, and promised to protect them from prosecution if it got exposed. (Matt 28:11-15)

Even though believers know the story well about the execution of Jesus and teach it carefully to their children, many simply don't believe what happened *then* can happen *now*. They deny or minimize the reality of the abuse of power by the state and law enforcement, even when there is actual video tape evidence to the contrary. How is that possible?

It is only possible when your life and theology are rooted in dominant culture power and privilege; when it is the default grid through which you view everything. You simply don't believe abuse and manipulation by those in power happens, because it has never happened to you. You jump to defend the system that has always worked for you, and you read the Bible through that lens. As Michelle Warren has said, "When you wake up every morning to a system that works for you, you feel it's a pretty good system."

On the other hand, when your life and theology are rooted in the context of oppression, poverty and exploitation, there is no need to expend effort conjuring up details about the abuse of power. They are daily all too familiar, and are obvious on nearly every page of the Bible.

When Sin Is More Than Personal

"You just need to be a flea against injustice. Enough committed fleas biting strategically can make even the biggest dog uncomfortable and transform even the biggest nation."
Marian Wright Edelman

I am puzzled by the push-back from many Christians at the recent exposure of blatant misconduct by law enforcement.

There seems to be a blanket acceptance by many conservative Christians that every action of law enforcement is justified, and that anyone who suggests law enforcement might be guilty of misconduct is rebelling against authority or doesn't believe in submission to God. Romans 13 which admonishes Christians to submit to those in authority over them is quoted a lot, and serves as the default justification for never questioning any violent encounter between law enforcement and citizens, especially citizens of color.

Are we so naïve as to believe those in power are incapable of abusing that power? The Old Testament prophets, as well as Jesus and the New Testament writers continually rail in nearly every chapter against power structures that abuse and exploit. If words mean anything, we must admit that the God of justice as described in Scripture is deeply concerned about justice and those who perpetrate injustice.

We certainly have seen blatant examples of abuse in arenas other than law enforcement. A lack of accountability over Wall Street, for example, created a culture that led to rampant abuse and financial collapse in 2008. Was every person on Wall Street corrupt? Of course not. Would anyone argue that it was wrong to expose the corruption in the Wall Street financial culture because, after all, there were "good men and women doing a good job there?"

The problem was that a culture of corruption was tolerated for so long that it led to collapse. It was a failure to address the problem that made it infinitely worse.

To refuse to admit that corruption could exist in an institution like law enforcement is simply naïve or a refusal to see. It will not do to argue from one's own personal experience that "the cops I know are good folks, and here are some examples of them doing good deeds!" That is a refusal to acknowledge the reality of institutional sin.

Thank God for those in law enforcement who serve and protect justly and fairly. To call out injustice in law enforcement is not a blanket condemnation of every policeman, any more than calling out political corruption is a condemnation of every politician, or calling out an embezzling accountant is a condemnation of every accountant, or calling out a cheating husband is a condemnation of all husbands.

We understand that when injustice is revealed in national organizations such as the VA, Catholic Church, Pennsylvania State University, Bob Jones University, Mission Agencies, and the NFL, it is not a condemnation of every person in those organizations. They all, however, must legally address cultures of non-accountability that led to corruption. To refuse to do so with that reality is to empower abusers.

Before God we cannot be selective in our condemnation of sin.

Polaroid Ministry

"'Jesus saw the poor and had compassion on them.'
To have compassion, you must first see."
Alexia Salvatierra

I came home on leave from the Army at Christmas, 1971, on a Greyhound bus. My family knew I was being transferred to Germany soon, would be gone for a while, and wanted me to have state-of-the-art equipment (!) to document my travels for them, so they gave me a Polaroid camera. No one in my family had ever been out of the country, so the idea of living in Europe was exotic and worthy of documenting.

One thing I soon learned from Polaroids; it takes time to see the whole picture. In the case of this archaic process, it was about 60 seconds. First a shadowy outline, gradually a few more details, some contrast after a while. Finally, eventually, the real picture emerged. Ah! That's what it was.

At any point before then, however, it was fuzzy and blurry, unintelligible. It wasn't that the picture wasn't there. It was. You just couldn't make it out right away. That took time.

A lot of things take time.

Those in dysfunctional and abusive relationships return to the abusive spouse an average of seven times before they actually leave permanently, if they leave at all.

Those in rehab program for addictions cycle through multiple times before they are able to escape addiction, if they escape it at all.

Victory is rarely clean; it consists of victories and setbacks, lurches forward and breathtaking, downward spirals.

I think of that process often in counseling, in discipling, in ministry, in teaching or preaching. Rarely does change happen instantly. It's tedious. Sometimes microscopic. It is sometimes hard to see right away.

As Brene Brown has said, sometimes Gods work is seen clearly, and sometimes you have to dust for fingerprints.

Patience.

VI. DEEP ROOTS

Expectations

"Expectations are disappointments under construction."
Anne Lamott

Guy: "Why is she always trying to re-make me into who she thinks I should be? Why can't she love me just for being me? Why this constant pressure to be different, to be someone else, like she's not happy with who I really am? What kind of a relationship is that? It's offensive."

Girl: "Why is he always trying to make me into someone different than who I am? I just wish I felt like he loved me for me. I don't though. I feel like he's always trying to re-cast me into the mold of who he thinks I should be. What kind of a relationship is that? It's offensive."

God: "Why do I always feel like you want to make me into someone different than who I really am? Why can't you love me for me, as I really am, rather than trying to re-cast me into the mold of who you think I should be? What kind of a relationship is that? It's offensive."

Slow Down

"In modern times, slowness is the new sickness."
Amit Kalantri

"A hundred and fifty years ago if we missed the stagecoach, it was alright. We just took the one next week. Today if we miss a section of a revolving door it throws our whole schedule off."

That statement haunts me simply because as a child of the times, I am the White Rabbit in Alice in Wonderland, always in a hurry and behind schedule:

> I'm late, I'm late, for a very important date,
> No time to say hello, goodbye,
> I'm late I'm late I'm late!

I'm late I'm late and when I wave
I lose the time I save.

Why do we feel the need to live at such a frantic pace? Jesus never traveled faster than 4 miles an hour. He never went farther than 60 miles from home. He was never interviewed on TV or radio, never wrote a book or blog post, never built a building, never used PowerPoint, Facebook or Twitter.

Yet, his impact was global, profound, and he fully accomplished the Father's will for his life.

Apparently God's evaluation of lifetime ministry impact is not calculated by how busy we are, how often or how broadly we travel, how big our budget is, how many followers we have on-line nor how many were in the service when we preached.

Maybe the point is for us to *be* before we *do*.

Who Is Fixing Whom?

"You care so much you feel as though you will bleed to death with the pain of it."
J.K. Rowling

The first time it happened in ministry I was devastated.

I was a young church planter in Germany among the military and had met a couple as I was doing house-to-house visitation in military housing areas. They were confessed Christians but adrift, and not really engaged anywhere. Something sparked relationally, and they ended up attending the church I pastored.

I invested a lot of time in them personally with marriage counseling, getting them growing and on-track spiritually; we spent time together in social contexts, invested relationally with their kids. We became good friends.

And then one day they just walked away from the faith. Without a word, they were gone. They stopped attending, stopped answering their phone. When I went to see them they spoke only at the door, were courteous but tight-lipped and distant. It was a phase, they had "moved on." They never talked to me again.

I was discouraged for weeks. How bad of a pastor am I? How did I fail so much in meeting their needs that they could just abandon the faith?

That was my introduction to a hard truth that I have lived with continually for forty years; pouring yourself out in ministry to people does not guarantee they will flourish and grow.

I have seen it also while working with those returning from incarceration who seemed to hold such promise, who finally seemed to have turned a corner in their lives. I have seen it with others who finally have victory over life-dominating sins. They are happy, they testify of what God has done in their lives, they want to be discipled, they serve now in various capacities in the church.

And then they walk away.

In my more cynical moments I have wondered if there is an inverse correlation between time invested in people and their spiritual stability and growth; the more you invest yourself in someone, the less likely they will flourish, the more likely it is they will drift way and wound you deeply in the process.

Such are a pastor's Monday morning thoughts.

Parents know that wound. Ask any group of parents about that reality and there will be an audible sigh and groan of recognition. Many will tell you of children who were raised in the faith, immersed in truth and a supportive, healthy youth group, kids who have been happy in Jesus and love the Bible, who have only known a stable family life, but who have now drifted far out to sea. Many can also tell you, through tears, the deep, intentional wounds they have received at the hand and lips of their children in order to justify their journey to a far country.

Many that we love the deepest, invest in most heavily and pray for the most fervently, seem to be the people who struggle the most and never really seem to make much spiritual headway. They seem to be the ones who, as we pour ourselves out beyond measure, most often kick us in the teeth and wound us deeply and relentlessly. We want so much for them, yet they experience so little of what we long for them to know.

Is it possible that we are not here for them so much, as they are here for us? Is it possible that God wants us to know more of what he experiences with humanity as he pours himself out so completely for us, yet receives such pain, rejection and indifference?

Maybe we who struggle with others in their continual cycle of pain and failure learn a bit more of the heart of God as he struggles with us. Maybe he doesn't expect us to fix everyone.

Maybe he is fixing us.

The Price of Ministry

"Deep suffering makes theologians of us all."
Barbara Brown Taylor

I discovered quite by accident today that Winston Churchill suffered from a fierce and chronic depression. Prompted me to reflect on what I know of another great leader's struggle.

Charles Spurgeon, the greatest English preacher of the last century was a full-time preacher for more than 40 years at the 5,000 member Metropolitan Tabernacle in London, but also suffered terribly from depression. On average, he missed 1 out of every 3 Sundays because he could not function.

In his lectures to his students he spoke of when he especially wrestled with depression:

1. The hour of great success. "When at last a long-cherished desire is fulfilled, when God has been glorified greatly by our means, a great triumph achieved, then we are apt to faint."

2. Before any great achievement. "An awful depression comes over me whenever the Lord is preparing a larger blessing for my ministry."

3. For seemingly no reason. "Causeless depression is not to be reasoned with.... If those who laugh at such melancholy did but feel the grief of it for one hour, their laughter would be sobered into compassion."

"My witness is, that those who are honored by their Lord in public have usually to endure or carry a secret chastening lest by any means they exalt themselves. The Refiner, though, is never far from the mouth of the furnace when the gold is in that fire, and the Son of God is always walking in the midst of the flames when His holy children are cast into them."

If you are a leader or aspire to be a leader, take note.

Doubt

"Doubts are the ants in the pants of faith.
They keep it awake and moving."
Fredrick Buechner

I was steeped for many years in an environment where any degree of doubt was an indicator of immature faith; the more faith you conjured up, the less doubt you would have. "God said it, I believe it, that settles it for me!" We said it and sang it. If you had doubts, you kept them to yourself. And maybe sang louder.

For some, certainty didn't even have to be about big theological issues, like whether God is real or if resurrection from the dead is possible. At its simplest level, those who apparently were really spiritual never seemed to doubt anything, big or small. They were certain someone would recover from sickness, that rent money would come from somewhere, or that a parking space would open up close to the entrance at the mall. People would exclaim at testimony time, "I just know that I know that I know!" and others would all smile approvingly.

I never felt that. It seemed so much like a conspiracy to agree publicly to something everyone knew wasn't true. Was something possible? Yes, OK, I could agree. But certain? Was everyone really so confident of everything? Was that the measure of our spirituality? No one ever seemed to request a de-brief when those things people were so certain would happen didn't, or the times others were so confident that something wouldn't happen, but did.

The fear of doubt had a different feel and emphasis in Christian higher education where I worked for twenty years. Author Phillip Yancey wrote that he was expected to sign a doctrinal statement yearly at a theological institution where he worked "without doubt or mental reservation." His response was that he could barely sign his own name without doubt or mental reservation. Was he the lone exception on the faculty?

Such attempts to stifle and eliminate doubt puts staffs and faculties in a practical and ethical quandary. Those who go along with the collective conspiracy to affirm every point of a doctrinal statement "with certainty, without doubt or mental reservation" stay employed. Many who feel the pressure of an ethical conundrum and have an internal aversion to such manipulation, find themselves searching for work.

It is a strange fear, in light of Paul's insistence in 2 Cor 5:7 that we walk by faith, not by sight. That of necessity entails some degree of doubt. To be absolutely certain of everything would be to have no need of faith. The opposite of faith is not doubt, it is certainty.

It seems reasonable, as Paul Tillich wrote, that doubt is not opposite of faith, but a part of faith. A significant part of deepening faith is wrestling with doubt; engaging new questions, teasing out new and deeper answers to old questions. There is never a time when we exhaust them all. Every time we answer one satisfactorily another pops up, much like a game of theological Whack-A-Mole.

Someone has described our dilemma of faith as an island surrounded by an ocean. The island contains that which we actually know for certain, the surrounding ocean everything that is unknown. The more we know the larger the island grows, but the larger the island grows the longer the shoreline becomes, the place where ignorance meets knowledge. If you wonder why you have more questions the older you get, that's why. You have a greater capacity for not knowing more things, a greater capacity to doubt.

We need not fear it. Doubt is not solved by closing our eyes tighter, or adding more propositional statements to a doctrinal statement. Faith means embracing the reality of doubt, and learning to trust in the dark as part of our deepening walk with a sovereign, good, loving God.

No Smell of Smoke

Not only were they not harmed, but there was no lingering effect, no smell of fire had come upon them.
(Daniel 3:27)

In one of the most familiar Scripture accounts, three young Hebrew boys go through a profoundly traumatic and difficult life ordeal. Threatened, intimidated, ultimately bound and thrown alive into a furnace (!) they are delivered unharmed. Astonishing to most anyone who does counseling, Scripture makes it clear they had no residual effects from their trauma:

Why some suffer from PTSD as a result of such events and others do not is a discussion for those more qualified than I. What is important to note, in my opinion, is that it is possible to survive profoundly difficult circumstances and come out stronger on the other side.

That is not to minimize responsibility or accountability for perpetrators of evil. It is simply an observation that in the midst of it all, victims do not have to abandon the faith as a result. Much like Joseph, they can ultimately say "You meant it for evil, but God meant it for good." (Gen 50:20)

Not all trauma is physical. For example, I have known and worked with some who have spent much of their lives in the strictest of Christian fundamentalist families, churches, and colleges, contexts that could have scarred them deeply both emotionally and spiritually. Surprisingly, they have no lingering trauma. There is no smell of smoke on their clothes. Somehow they have managed to walk away intact.

It has not been painless, but they are not bitter or resentful. They are deeply grateful for some things; they came to know Jesus in those circles, they came to learn and love the Bible there, to serve others, they learned to see the value of church even with all of its glaring flaws. As country folk used to say, they took the corn and left the cob.

These are white, middle class, former fundamentalists who now have a deep commitment to the poor, immigrants and refugees; they bleed empowerment and development as a philosophy of ministry, they engage heavily with justice and race issues. They have broadened their theological framework, they have moved into urban, multiethnic neighborhoods, put their children in urban schools, thrown themselves fully into school board issues for the betterment of education for all; they have marched in protest in Ferguson, protested against police misconduct here in Denver. They are former fundamentalists who, in their previous lives, would have argued and stood against all of that.

I know them personally. We are friends. Although many of us feel like we are still in recovery from our fundamentalist backgrounds and have the scars to prove it, their testimony is a powerful one; it is possible to move on and flourish. You can live, thrive and serve in freedom and joy without the smell of fundamentalist smoke in your clothes.

Saying Goodbye

"Ever has it been that love knows not its own depth until the hour of separation."
Kahlil Gibran

October, 2013. One week from tonight we will say goodbye to our children and grandchildren. We leave for Denver a week from tomorrow.

On the one hand, we are so excited. God has called us. It is clear. We could never turn back. On the other hand, this week is going to be tough. If you pray, pray for us this week.

Do you know how painfully slow the clock ticks over when you have a set time to leave those you love? That's how slowly time will drag this week. Every day, every passing moment, every meal, every laugh, every shared memory, every hug, every cell phone picture together comes with an awareness of what looms. This must be what death row feels like.

We have been here before. It never gets easier. The clock will tick down to the last day, the last visit, the last meal. After dinner the conversation will buzz for a while, then gradually dwindle, grow quieter. More reflective. People will transition from reminiscing about the past to talking about the future. Everyone will write, yes. Call? Of course. Facebook? Naturally. Skype? Yes, we'll learn.

And then, eventually, that time will come. We will stand, reluctantly, and look into those teary eyes that we have looked into since birth. We will hug and hang on. Kiss those precious babies. Say goodbye through tears. Pray. Eventually, when we must, we will inch our way to the car. More hugs. More tears. More promises through car windows.

They will all stand under the porch light and wave, probably until long after we are out of sight. And then, they will all go inside to a different life.

And we will drive off to a different life.

Sometimes this following Jesus business is tough.

Ministry Is Hard

Jesus made the disciples get into the boat and sent them to the other side…. and the wind was against them.
(Mark 6:45-47)

What makes us think if Jesus is in it, it won't be hard? And if it is hard, Jesus must not be in it?

Jesus made his disciples get into the boat, and then sent them into a storm. It was their obedience that caused their difficulties.

In 1978 I was a staff sergeant in charge of 270 men when I was discharged from the Army after seven years to prepare for ministry. As a lowly, 26 year-old first-semester freshman in college I took the only job I could get, scraping rust off of outdoor equipment with a wire brush and spray painting oil paint while standing on a 40 foot ladder inside a sweltering hot foundry for minimum wage. It was awful and humbling. I deeply wanted to serve Jesus in ministry, and he gave me a wire brush, a difficult boss and a back-breaking ladder.

Four years later after I graduated from college and went to seminary, the only job I could get was working at an iron foundry pouring molten iron for just above minimum wage in sweltering Indiana heat. It also was awful, the worst job on the planet, worse than the infantry. I desperately wanted to serve Jesus in ministry, he sent me to an iron foundry.

After seminary, we felt God calling us to missions in Germany. We ended up spending two years on the road preaching and raising financial support, driving thousands of miles, sleeping in people's spare bedrooms and basements with two small children, pitching the vision for church planting among the American military in over a hundred churches. I wanted to pastor, he put us on the road in a used station wagon with two small children in tow.

We did eventually end up pastoring for ten years in Europe, and then for the next twenty years I served both as a staff pastor and taught at a university in the U.S.

Following that God loosened our tent pegs and called us back into urban missions in Denver. This time finances were not the challenge, it was leaving our children and grandchildren behind at age 58 to move across the country. We had never not all lived in the same city. Pulling away in a U-Haul truck in tears and waving in the rear-view mirror to everyone that meant something to us was another level of trauma. We wanted our lives to count for Jesus in our twilight years, but we drove away in a moving van leaving behind those we loved the most.

In hindsight, from the depths of our hearts we can say that, although profoundly difficult, each stage and each crisis resulted in the deepest, most fulfilling experience and the next level of intimacy with God.

But only in hindsight. Beforehand, we were like Jacob wrestling with the angel. It was hand to hand combat with what God was asking us to do. Painful. Difficult. Impossible. But as we pried our fingers off the steering wheel and yielded control by faith, we found grace and God. We say now, with full confidence and resolve, it was worth it at every stage. Really.

You cannot reason your way there, in my opinion. You must act your way there. By faith.

The deepest blessing of God is always on the other side of commitment.

Dark Night of the Soul

"If we never experience the chill of a dark winter, it is very unlikely that we will ever cherish the warmth of a bright summer's day."
Anthon St. Marten

It was awful, but we did it anyway. We left him alone and walked away. He was sobbing desperately, pleading for us not to leave. We did what we had to do though. We left.

We only went about ten feet. We hovered right outside of his bedroom door, praying desperately that he would calm himself and go to sleep. Not a chance. At the tender age of 3 he was convinced his parents were abandoning him.

Why would a young boy loved by his parents think such a thing? Because he couldn't see us, feel us, or sense our closeness. When we walked out of that room, he reasoned, we were gone, probably forever.

A hard life lesson when you're 3, this business of trusting what you can't see. It was scary on his part, emotionally exhausting for us. Learning to trust and function apart from evidence of the physical, visible, assuring presence of those they love is part of every child's journey of becoming self-sufficient. Until they learn to trust in the dark what they have learned in the light, they remain clingy, paralyzed with insecurities and fearful of everything.

When they finally do learn to trust in what they can't see, an amazing, broad world of adventure opens up. Overnights at grandma's house, trips to the zoo with cousins, Sunday school, field trips with school friends and a kaleidoscope of other experiences are all undertaken with a new underlying sense of confidence and assurance. They know they are still loved and cared for by people they love, even though they can't physically see or feel them. To be untethered from the paralyzing fear of abandonment is a profoundly significant benchmark in the life of a child.

Sometimes, because as parents we know how important this lesson is, we are wise enough to orchestrate the painful circumstances that will force them to learn it.

Such is God's relationship with us.

The early church fathers called it the 'dark night of the soul,' this deep sense of abandonment by God, silence, the feeling of absence, distance, the overwhelming panic that he no longer is here. Such experiences of withdrawal, in fact, are orchestrated from time to time by God himself. It is an act of love. He wants us to experience what it is like to feel that he is distant. Absent. Why? Not because he actually is, but because he wants to wean us from dependence on our feelings for our relationship with him.

Certainly he delights in fostering those times with us when he is palpably close, times that are an inexpressible and deep joy. But then, as a good parent, he also wants us to learn to trust him by faith apart from feelings and emotions. He knows we must learn to trust him in the dark, during long stretches of time when we can't see or feel him. There will be times when we pray and there is no answer, times when we cry out to him in desperation and he is silent.

C. S. Lewis lamented the silence of God after the death of his wife, when God seemed to withdraw at the very point he would have expected just the opposite:

"...if you remember yourself and turn to Him with gratitude and praise, you will be — or so it feels— welcomed with open arms. But go to Him when your need is desperate, when all other help is vain, and what do you find? A door slammed in your face, and a sound of bolting and double bolting on the inside. After that, silence."

— C.S. Lewis, A Grief Observed

Jesus groans the same sentiment from the depth of his being in the Garden: "My God, My God, why have you forsaken me?" That is not the desperate cry of an atheist, but a deep, gut-wrenching expression from the depths of one deeply committed to God who feels at the core of his being an awful sense of abandonment.

This must inform our thinking when we find ourselves immersed in darkness that seems inescapable. If at some point your own soul has cried out the same prayer of Jesus, just know: God has not abandoned you. He is close, outside the bedroom door, waiting for you to stop panicking and to rest in faith, even though you can't see or feel him.

He longs for you to trust him in the dark. He has not abandoned you.
He will not. Ever.

Team Player

*Now there are varieties of gifts, but the same Spirit. All these are
empowered by one and the same Spirit, who apportions to each one
as he wills.*
(I Corinthians 12:4,11)

I stumbled onto a particular truth about ministry recently and felt
slightly embarrassed that I had not recognized or acknowledged it
before now. It is this:

"I am most likely to be impatient and critical of others in those areas
where I am gifted."

Not exactly a spectacular blaze of insight, but it's true. I am
wired/gifted by God as an encourager. That comes naturally to me. I
affirm those around me as naturally as breathing. I don't have to work
at it. I don't have to conjure up things in some veiled attempt to
manipulate through flattery. Sometimes verbally, often in writing, I see
and try to affirm people in ways that, hopefully, strengthen and build
their confidence, faith and character.

The problem comes when I take my area of giftedness and impose it
on others. What's the big deal, I think. Why don't others speak up
when they see things to affirm? People are so self-centered. They just
don't care about others. Such a small thing to encourage and affirm.
They act like affirming others costs them money. Etc. etc. etc.

Wait a minute.

I am realizing that what God has given to me as a gift can become a
club, a default means of judging and criticizing, of dividing and
questioning others spirituality. It's unhealthy, destructive, and
decidedly unfair. I don't like people imposing their giftedness as a
standard for me, and so shouldn't do so with others.

Those whose gift of evangelism spills out everywhere must be careful not to judge the spirituality of the rest of us because our every conversation doesn't lead to talking about Jesus. Those with the gift of mercy must not become critics of all of us who do not naturally gravitate towards suffering. Givers must be wary of becoming experts not only in giving but in judgment of others, and leaders careful not to allow their natural ability to influence to poison their perception of everyone else not so gifted.

I can spend all of my time criticizing others for not being like me. *Or,* I can play my position, you can play yours, everyone else can play theirs, and we could make a pretty good team.

Leaving Church

"Quietly turning the backdoor key, stepping outside, she is free."
Lyrics to "She's Leaving Home." - The Beatles

Often we here in the West haven't made the faith too difficult – we've made it too easy. We've set the bar too low. People are hungry to invest their lives in something bigger than they are, something that makes a difference, something that is transformational to people and society in the name of Jesus.

All we've often done, though, is tell people to manage their hormones, don't get drunk on the weekend, be nice, and be in your seat when the show starts.

And we wonder why people bail out of the church.

People aren't leaving the church because they have lost their faith, they are leaving the church in order to preserve their faith. When we help people engage a broken world instead of simply sit in a service, people come alive in their commitment to Jesus.

That's not radical. That's the normal Christian life.

Throwing Good Money After Bad

"Don't be afraid to make mistakes. But if you do, make new ones. Life is too short to make the wrong choice twice."
Joyce Rachelle

It was a tough lesson.

The car looked great and was advertised at a great price. When I went to see it on my lunch break I couldn't believe my eyes. An old man owned it and probably hadn't driven it much in the last 15 years. A steal. "Let me just drive it around the block to check it out," I said.

"Oh, I don't dare," he said. "The brakes are really bad, but other than that you can see it's in great shape." It certainly looked like it.

I prayed about it, considered the wisdom of buying a car without driving it, but it was a steal, and he was a nice old man. I gave him $200 (This was 40 years ago!), and inched down the street towards the inspection station across town. It certainly needed brakes.

In Kansas you had to get a safety inspection first to get plates, and there they told me, to my astonishment, that it needed not just brakes, but over $1,000 of other repairs to get it to pass inspection. That was far more than it was worth. I was sick.

I wrestled with the decision. Should I just go ahead with the repairs? I had already come this far with the deal. I was already committed to the stupid thing.

Nope. After a bit of introspection, I drove it from the inspection station straight to a junkyard, and they gave me $50 for it. I went back to work, $150 poorer, still with no car.

Not a good lunch break.

Life lesson: When you make a bad decision, own it. Learn from it. Don't *keep* making bad decisions to try and fix the first one.

That is not just a lesson about buying cars.

All I've Got

"Never once did Jesus scan the room for the best living and send that person out to tell others about him. He always sent stumblers and sinners. I find that comforting."
Nadia Bolz-Weber

"What's that in your hand, Moses?"
"A stick."
"Let me show you something," says God.

"What do you have left in the house to eat?"
"Not much. A little oil and a handful of barley."
"Let me show you something," says Elijah.

"What do you have in that basket, son?"
"A couple of fish and some bread."
"Let me show you something," says Jesus.

Notice any patterns?

1. God is not asking us for what we don't have.
2. He knows that none of us have much to offer. A stick. A little oil. A fish or two.
3. He delights in using unremarkable people with few resources to accomplish the profound.

Feeling insignificant? Convinced he has no use for you? Nothing to offer?

Perfect. Just offer yourself.

"What do you have?" he asks.
"Here. Let me show you something."

Traveling the Back Roads

"I have learned things in the dark that I could never have learned in the light, things that have saved my life over and over again, so that

*there is really only one logical conclusion. I need darkness as much
as I need light."*
Brene Brown

My youngest daughter and I were laughing so hysterically we almost
wrecked the car.

I had just remarked how good God was because her older sister Emily
had just graduated with her Masters in Nursing on Saturday, married a
great guy on Sunday, and gotten hired into a great hospital nursing job
on Tuesday.

"OK," Natalie said. "She's gonna have to tell me *exactly* what she said
to God to make that happen!"

"She is so funny!" I told my wife later. I posted our exchange on
Facebook, and apparently a lot of people thought it was funny too.

I have since that time wondered, however, how many perhaps didn't
laugh so hard. You know, those who not only didn't get a ring by
spring, but the ones with no one even on the horizon. Those who
graduated a year ago but are still working at Wal-Mart or Starbuck's
trying to find a job in their field. Those whose education is on hold,
again, because of finances. No exciting job, no family gathering to
celebrate a graduation, no awesome wedding.

For many, they are trapped in the movie Groundhog Day. Another day
all over again.

Ever been there? Ever have that conversation in your head, "What's
wrong with me? How come good things don't ever come my
way? Why is it always other people?"

There is another part to Emily's story. She would gladly tell you the
back-story.

First, she's not 22, she's 31.

Yes, she was married on Sunday to a great guy. But the last five years
have been profoundly lonely after she was divorced by her first
husband. For five, seemingly-interminable years she despaired of ever

meeting anyone again, of ever having a family. Facebook was filled with other glowing reports and pictures of people dating, getting married, having babies. For her, though, no one ever came along. Ever. No calls. No interest. Not even a coffee date.

Some of the most emotionally painful times for me as a father have been those conversations in past years where she has shared through tears, "Dad, it is so discouraging to come home every night to an empty house. To have nobody. It is just so lonely. To have nothing to look forward to but work." And there was nothing I could do about it.

That went on for five years.

Yes, she was hired into a new job this week, just two days after her wedding. It is indeed a gift of God. But the back story is, with no other job on the horizon she resigned from her previous job for her health and a variety of other reasons. She could tell you of the fear and uncertainty of being in a position of having to trust God when nothing was happening, when resumes went out by the score but no one even returned calls, let alone wanted an interview. It was scary.

Yes, she graduated with her Masters in Nursing on Saturday. But she could recount for you the years she worked consistently and relentlessly, weekends and weeknights. Mt. Everest was climbed, it seemed, one halting baby-step at a time, one class at a time, one semester at a time.

Has it been a great weekend of celebrations? Absolutely! Graduation? Wedding? Honeymoon? Move to a new house? New job? It has been astonishing, fun to watch and experience.

But, lest some think that wonderfully exciting and fulfilling things fall easily and regularly into the laps of everyone else all of the time and God for unknown reasons always ignores you, know this; things don't just "happen." These times are not accidents. There is no secret and precise wording of a prayer that gets God to relent and deliver fantastic life experiences for some.

The reality is, there are back-story roads that all of us must travel that are long, hard, dusty and often discouraging. It is the back stories that we live that eventually lead us to those breathless, exclamation-mark-filled Facebook entries about jobs, graduations, weddings and babies.

Take heart! The journey precedes the arrival. Your time will come.

Sometimes He Delivers

"How do we develop the courage to walk in the dark if we are never asked to practice?"
Barbara Brown Taylor

One of the hardest truths to accept in the Christian life is one that is clearest in Scripture.

We wish it weren't true. If only God would have asked me, I would have been glad to advise him and suggest several alternatives, one's that were a little more positive. You know, to keep us all happy. Ah, if only.

He didn't.

The hard truth is this: Sometimes God delivers. Sometimes God delivers miraculously. Sometimes God delivers miraculously in answer to the prayers of his people. And sometimes he does not.

And it has nothing to do with their faith.

Hebrews 11 recounts familiar stories of those who saw miraculous acts of deliverance, astonishing events where God stepped in and supernaturally showed off. Noah! Abraham! Sarah! Moses! God executing his power in unmistakably divine ways.

People pray! God delivers! People praise Him and testify of his deliverance!

No mistaking it. God is good.

"But others…" (11:35) Ah, there's the rub. "But others were tortured, flogged, chained, put in prison, stoned, sawn in two, put to death by the sword…"

Question: What was the matter with *their* faith?

Answer: Nothing. Sometimes people of faith pray and God delivers. And sometimes he does not. Sometimes we cry out to God in absolute and total surrender, faithfully trusting him and him alone in desperate circumstances and he delivers. At other times, he sits on his hands. In silence. And he does not.

There is the testing ground. Do we believe that God is still good and still intends good for us, even when we don't know what he is doing?

That is what faith looks like: trusting God in the dark when we can't see the way ahead, what he is doing, and fog engulfs everything. We have no answer but faith.

Show Us Something New?

In the future, when your children ask you, "What do these stones mean?" you can tell them they remind us…
(Joshua 4:6-7)

"Lord show us something new in the Scriptures today."

I have often prayed that way, and heard others pray that way. Yet, I have begun to question recently what I actually mean when I say that. It has begun to strike a bit of a dissonant chord in my spirit. Here's why.

Is it reasonable to expect that every time I read the Bible I will find something new, something exciting that I had not known before? Will some new information be added to my theological knowledge base, a previously unknown insight discovered that will make me a stronger, more consistent, more mature husband, father, follower of Jesus?

I ask myself if that would be a reasonable expectation in any other relationship. Should I expect to discover something new, exciting and unknown every time I talk to my wife? Is every interaction with my children, my boss, my co-workers a gateway to insightful discoveries about them?

"What a disappointing time!" I might say to myself on the way home from a wonderful candlelight dinner with my wife. "There must be something wrong between us. We just spent some great time together but I don't feel like I learned anything new."

Perhaps an important part of deeply meaningful relationships that are healthy and growing is a regular rehearsal of the familiar, a reflection on what we already know and cherish and embrace. Perhaps in our pursuit of the new, we are too quick to devalue the role of familiarity in our relationship with God.

In every other relationship I have, there is rich value in rehearsing, retelling and even re-living common knowledge and experiences. It bonds us more deeply together. Why would I expect my relationship with God to only flourish with what is new?

Of course there will be flashes of new insight, times of new growth from fresh knowledge gained. But is it realistic to expect such experiences every time I crack open the Bible? I think not.

Maybe when God and I just spend time together, it's a good thing.

Paying Attention

"Your life does change as you get older. You get into what's important and what's not."
Ashton Applewhite

My experience is, if you pay attention in life, you will learn some things. You will also unlearn some things. At age 62, this is where I am:

I am *more convinced* than ever that:

- grace is a quiet and deep gift of infinite worth.
- the *worst* people who have done the most horrific things can still be redeemed.
- the *best* followers of Jesus have glaring, astonishing flaws.
- God loves to love. I don't know why he does me.
- Jesus knows every one of my flaws, and embraces me still.
- the life of faith and maturity is not produced or enhanced by learning doctrinal positions or secret handshakes. It is a deeply subjective work of the Spirit and Jesus, unique to each.
- God resists attempts to categorize/diagram him.
- the family of God is much broader than I think.
- community is the non-optional context for spiritual formation.
- God will get us where he wants us to be.

I am *less convinced* than ever:

- of rigid and systematized categories of theology.
- that right information and doctrinal stance is the key to maturity and character.
- that the Bible needs to be defended.
- that every theological hill is worth dying on.
- that all problems can be solved by obedience to the Word. Some problems will only be fixed on the other side.
- that any one theological camp has the corner on the market of Truth.

Not comprehensive, obviously, but stuff that is pretty high on the list of things imprinted in my DNA over the years.

Twenty One Principles for Living

If 21 is the magic number for maturity, here are 21 life principles to get there:

1. Stop letting your feelings control your life. Feelings are real, they're just not authoritative. If feelings are the driving force behind your decisions you are in for a rough ride.

2. Buck up. You are not the first person to ever have difficult times come your way. Calm seas never made great captains. Keep your eyes on Jesus, not on the waves. If you think you are the only one who has ever gone through what you are going through, you are not paying attention. If you collapse into a puddle of tears and drown in discouragement every time you hit a rough spot in life you won't do much. Find your backbone.

3. Knuckle down. Stuff in life doesn't come your way just because you show up. Most things in life you don't get by accident. Want a relationship to work? College education? Lose weight? Run a marathon? Things happen because you went after it. Relentlessly.

4. Adjust. Things may not work out 100% as you planned. Some things may not work out at all. Plan on it. Grieve as necessary. Adjust accordingly.

5. Stop whining. It's not attractive in children or adults. Remember your greatest ministry flows out of your deepest pain.

6. Lean into your fears. If fear is in the driver's seat of your life, you won't do much. Risk is not a curse word.

7. Be a team player. You need others. Others need you. Affirm people a lot.

8. Clean up your messes. Relational and otherwise.

9. Be solution oriented, not problem oriented. Stop endlessly re-hashing your problems and fixing blame. Work through stuff and come out on the other side.

10. Stop expecting everyone else to make your life happy or meaningful or complete. You are responsible for you.

11. Invest in other people. Stop being so selfish. It's amazing what comes your way from the overflow.

12. Listen and learn, especially from those different than you. Keep reminding yourself that you don't know everything about everything.

13. Tune your internal radar for the lonely, marginalized, and invisible. God takes notice.

14. Learn how to fail. Don't make perfection an idol. You will fail. Expect it. Learn from it. Fail forward. Ask forgiveness when it hurts others.

15. Take the job you can get until you get the job you want. Most people start out entry level. Welcome to the club. Pay your dues.

16. Deny yourself something regularly just for the self-discipline. Stuff is the crack cocaine of the middle class. Learn to say no to yourself, not because something is wrong but because you need a stronger will. That only comes with exercising it.

17. Push yourself to pursue a challenge that's bigger than you are. Get a degree? Doctorate? Get involved with a critical social issue? Scuba-dive? Bike across the U.S.? Write a book? Stop talking about what you are going to do and do it. The woods are full of 'big talkers' and all that they are going to do. Be unique. Do something.

18. If you have dug yourself in to a deep hole, here is step # 1: stop digging.

19. Stop being so critical. Learn to give grace. Allow others the freedom to grow and to fail.

20. Let God tell you who you are. No one else.

21. Remember that getting out of bed is not the hardest thing you will ever do.

Afterword

If I had another lifetime I would devote it all to the study of history.

Unless we grasp a broad panoramic sweep of history, we tend to be prisoners trapped in an echo chamber reverberating continuously with the limited perspectives of our own age and milieu. We are not alone, of course. We are trapped and surrounded by others with limited views and perspectives as well.

A deep grasp of historical perspective can do much to temper the arrogance of the age that arises when we believe our narrow perspective is the only right one, indeed, the only one possible. My own journey has been an attempt to escape the echo chamber in which I have found myself.

To pursue such a trajectory as a Christian is not a freefall into "liberalism," as is often the charge by those on the extreme edges of conservatism. Even a cursory view of the historical landscape demonstrates that the past is littered with embarrassing examples of what happens when the Church disregards its own echo chamber, uses the Bible for justification and marries the wisdom of the age. For example, the following were taught and defended as biblical positions at various points in history:

- The earth is flat
- The earth is the center of the universe
- Black people are cursed by God
- Slavery is biblical and ordained by God
- Annihilation of Native Americans was the will of God
- Apartheid/segregation is biblical
- The church should not get involved in social issues

It is a grief and deep embarrassment that the Church has on more than one occasion found itself on the wrong side of history and the Bible. It has often had to repent; sometimes of its arrogance, sometimes of its naivete. It is familiar territory; I have often had to do that as well.

In light of this, the overarching question for me as I have grown older and hopefully somewhat wiser, is this: "What positions do we now staunchly defend as biblical, but fifty years from now will be an embarrassment to the cause of Christ?"

That is not an easy question, but it is a necessary one. It is a question that individuals as well as the Church must continuously ask. It is that question over the years that has moved me in fits and spurts along a continuum to a broader, more holistic, more robust stance towards life, theology and ministry that is reflected in the book you have just read.

It will not do to say that Christians or the Church inevitably drift towards liberalism when positions change, unless we are willing to argue that a flat earth, slavery and geo-centrism were biblical moorings that we have forsaken. On the contrary, the Church has often become more biblical when its views have adapted and changed. To be a follower of Jesus, in fact, is to be deeply committed to change.

That is not a call for the Church to be set adrift, or that everything is relative. It *is* a call, however, in light of our track record in history, for followers of Jesus to be a little more tentative, a little more humble and a little more informed when speaking for God and insisting "this is what the Bible says." It also is a call to be a little bit more desirous of plumbing the depths of what it means to flourish in our life with God.

God has been kind and patient with me and those like me who have fumbled our way along in a life of discovery, and who also by his grace continue to pursue a deeply satisfying, flourishing, authentic life. The learning curve has been steep, but as Maya Angelou once said about her life, "I did then what I knew how to do. When I knew better, I did better."

Such is our goal as followers of Jesus. My prayer is that this book has moved the needle a bit and enabled us to know better and do better.

Acknowledgements

I am deeply indebted to my dear friend and former university student Kristi Graydon who spent countless hours scouring social media, collecting and editing these entries that I have written over the past several years. Without her willingness to tackle such a tedious task I would have had neither the will, patience nor technological expertise to attempt this collection. Your reward shall be great in heaven!

Thank you for your labor of love, sweet friend.